T0106033

Teen girlfriends

Teen girlfriends

Celebrating the Good Times, Getting through the Hard Times

Julia DeVillers

Introduction by
Carmen Renee Berry & Tamara Traeder

WILDCAT CANYON PRESS
A Division of Circulus Publishing Group, Inc.
Berkeley, California

Teen girlfriends: Celebrating the Good Times, Getting through the Hard Times

Editorial Director: Roy M. Carlisle
Marketing Director: Carol Brown
Managing Editor: Leyza Yardley
Production Coordinator: Larissa Berry
Cover Design: Saffron Creative
Interior Design: Margaret Copeland
Typesetting: Margaret Copeland/Terragraphics
Typographic Specifications: Body text set in Cochin, 11/15. Heads set in Enviro and Impress BT.

Printed in the United States of America

Cataloging-in-Publication Data
DeVillers, Julia.
    Teen girlfriends / by Julia DeVillers ; introd. by Carmen Renee
    Berry & Tamara Traeder.
        p. cm.
    Includes bibliographical references.
    Summary: Interviews with more than 100 teenage girls provide a
    look at various aspects of friendship between young women.
        ISBN 1-885171-52-8 (alk. paper)
        1. Teenage girl—Juvenile literature. 2. Friendship in adolescence—
    Juvenile literature. 3. Female frienship—Juvenile literature. [1.
    Frienship. 2. Teenage girls.] I. Title.

HQ798.D399 2001
305.235—dc21   2001026559

Distributed to the trade by Publishers Group West
10 9 8 7 6 5 4 3 2   01 02 03 04 05

Contents

Dedication

To my twin sister,
Jennifer Rozines Roy,
girlfriend from the very beginning.

Acknowledgments

Thank you! to the teens who so enthusiastically contributed their stories to this book. You are wise, witty, and extremely fun. And I thank the parents of these teens, who have been so supportive throughout the process.

An enormous thank you! to Carmen Renee Berry and Tamara Traeder for their inspiration.

My husband, David, has been a source of great support and encouragement since we met as teenagers ourselves. Special thanks to my daughter, Quinn, who sat at her pre-school-sized desk next to mine, keeping me company in "our" home office. I took a respite from writing this book to welcome Jack Hamilton DeVillers into the world, and I am grateful for his joyous personality. More thanks go to Robin Rozines, the ultimate mom, and to my sister, Amy Rozines (particularly for the stay in Scottsdale to celebrate the completion of the manuscript).

Writing this book brought up many memories of my own teen girlfriends—Jacki Watson, Carol Burke, Melanie DeLorme, and Sue Beckwith—from my Oswego days. I am fortunate to still call them friends.

I'd like to acknowledge the contribution of Johanna Haney for her fabulous, as always, editorial assistance. Others who contributed in some shape or form include Dawn Nocera, Molly Simpson at CSG, Linda Meeks, Debra Pack, Lori Rossi-Barrett, Dawn DeVillers, Robin

Fisher Roffer, my elementary school teacher Nancy Guest, and professor Janet Hickman.

A very special thanks to the teen cover "models"— Nora Barich and Helen Feldman, Beckie Ninnis and Stephanie Melton, Melissa Tirendi and Alyssa Schreiner, and Michalea Delaveris and Megan Kauffman.

And thank you! to the exceptional Wildcat Canyon team, Carol Brown, Leyza Yardley, Patsy Barich, Nenelle Bunnin, Larissa Berry, and Priscilla Call. And I am indebted to Roy M. Carlisle. Thank you, Roy, for the opportunity.

Introduction

Friends: they mean the world to us. Where would we be without their listening ears, their advice, their ability to make us laugh? Our friends hold us up when the pace of life becomes overwhelming. With them, we laugh wildly, think deeply, and feel we are not alone in the world. We have pillow fights, have phone-a-thons, and share clothes with them. Our friends make us believe in ourselves. They tap our inner resources and bring out the best in us. They empower us with their unconditional love. And, perhaps most importantly, they are unhesitatingly there for us, no matter when or where we are.

We use the term "girlfriend" to describe our best, most crucial friendships. When Julia defined the phrase to the girls who responded to her surveys, they immediately knew which of their friends ranked in the "girlfriends" category. You might have many types of friends, but your girlfriends are the truest, closest, and most beloved.

When she asked what was the best thing about having girlfriends, you overwhelmingly responded: "They get it." You love to listen to what your friends have to say and, possibly even more, you love when they listen to you. Suppose you had the most unbelievable day. You made the team, *he* asked you to be his lab partner, or you snagged a couple tickets to the sold-out show. It almost seems unreal; it's too good to be true. Then your phone rings. It's your girlfriend. You curl up on the bed and tell her your news. She shrieks and celebrates and grills you with questions, dissecting the most minute of details. Relating every gory detail is almost as good as the experience itself. And now that you have shared it with her, the experience is officially real.

"My mother asked me why Elaine and I are such close friends," says Joy. "I tried to explain to her that having someone to be close to who's going through the same kinds of physical and emotional changes as you are is important. One reason Elaine and I are so close is because we know that we are connected by our age. Major changes are occurring during the teenage years. You're becoming an adult. What you need then is someone who is just as confused as you are by new responsibilities, thoughts of getting good grades, a boyfriend, a job. My connection with Elaine, and all my other friends, is not just a simple enjoyment with each other, but a connection over growing up."

Sara Shandler writes in *Ophelia Speaks*: "During adolescence, friends bring an intimate quality of support that can't be provided by any adult. The comfort of our peer connections is reflected in our most honest and direct hand-holding. When we trip, they are the first ones to pull us up."[1]

And we all need to be pulled up at times. The teen years are a tumultuous period. Hormones are raging, bodies are changing, you're making your way into the world.

Adolescence is a time of radical changes. And it is particularly complex in today's world. Violence, drugs, gangs, divorce, and stepfamilies surround us. Pressure to get good grades, be stick thin, and be in with the guys nearly suffocates us. We're bombarded with information from the countless teen magazines beckoning to us from the newsstand to the millions of web sites just waiting for a hit. Our girlfriends can help us make our way through this fast-paced and sophisticated world, steering us safely through the treacherous waters known as the teenage years. A girlfriend can reaffirm that there is good in the world, and in us. Together, we become women.

We learn about ourselves through our friendships. What do we like? What do we dislike? What are we really like, deep inside? We define ourselves as we examine our friends' behavior and the intricacies of our relationships with them. Being a friend teaches us lessons that make us better people: we learn to be loyal, patient, empathetic, and compassionate. We learn the qualities we admire and respect in people. We might look different, come from different backgrounds, and have different talents, but friendship can transcend differences and open up new worlds for us as we gain a new and wider perspective on life.

Friendships come in all shapes and sizes, colors, and flavors. We have friends we talk to so much that, if a day passes without a conversation with them, we have Girlfriend

Withdrawal. We have friends that we see only once a year, but each time we see them it is as if no time has passed at all. As Allison says, "There are so many different types of girlfriends! You have best friends, with whom you do everything, and those people that you just say 'hi' to in the hallway sometimes who you don't even remember where you know them from. I even have a hair-dye friend! We usually don't hang out with each other, but we get together when one of us wants to change our hair color."

We learn early on that we have different friends for our different needs. Four-year-old Quinn puts it this way: "Sara Nicole is my best friend. Annamarie is my friend that is like my sister. Julia is my school friend. Justine is my playing Barbies friend. Meagan is my friend I can see in her windows and wave to her. Dorothy from the *Wizard of Oz* seems like my friend, even if she is just pretend." And when we get older, our friends continue to meet our different needs, but the categories change. Trinity describes them as such: "I have best friends, friends who care, friends who don't. Friends who are totally straight edge and friends who aren't. Friends who are wild and friends who are mellow. People I talk to only online and people who hate to talk online. Friends who are really smart and friends who don't care about school. I have friends who will always be there when bad stuff happens to me, and those who celebrate the good stuff."

Our different kinds of friendships fulfill different aspects of ourselves. We might have a best friend or a group of best friends. Activity friends, such as those who take dance lessons or play ball with us, share our common interests. E-mail friends and long-distance friends allow us to get to know other people outside our own comfort zones. Some friends have been with us as long as we can remember. Others are brand new, but prove themselves worthy of the girlfriend label almost instantly. A friend who seems peripheral suddenly steps in at a time of need and goes beyond the call of duty. Our friendships are fluid and ever changing. Our groups change and friends float in and out of our lives, but the impact they have on us is immeasurable.

We recognize that friends come and go. We've all been through painful "friend breakups" and had friendships that just drifted apart. But we hold tightly to other friends and envision being, as so many of you say, FF — Friends Forever. We know that some friendships can overcome time, distance, and changes to last throughout lifetimes.

Moon imagines a future with her friend: "We will be sitting in rocking chairs, with our grandkids biting at our ankles, asking us stories about what it was like growing up in the 1900s. And we'll look at them and hope that they, too, have relationships as tight as the two of us will have had for decades."

This book is not a lecture, there is no preaching. The author is not a teenager and doesn't pretend to be. She's not going to give you the line, "I understand, I've been a teenager myself," because adolescence has changed dramatically since the last generation. This book consists of selections of interviews with more than a hundred teens, and it reflects what you have to say.

Anyone who believes that teenage friendships are not as heartfelt as their older counterparts will be surprised when they read what you have to say. "She is my soul mate." "I love her more than life itself." "She means the world to me." Teen girls are fiercely loyal to their friends, and bestow upon true friends an exalted status. Teens appreciate their friends dearly, and they are vocal about sharing their feelings. The response to this book was overwhelming. Teens who responded to the surveys asked for more questions, more time to think of answers, and continued to call and e-mail with more and more stories. It became clear that teens want to publicly rejoice in the friendships they have. They begged to include messages to their friends in the book: "Love ya, Brittany!" "Can you put in it: Elena, you're the best!?" We believe that those messages come through loud and clear in the stories that follow. This book is a tribute to all teenage girls—present and past—who have, and are, a girlfriend.

—*Carmen Renee Berry*
Tamara Traeder

Exploring Friendship

There is no particular rule book for making a friend. We don't wear a badge saying "Friends Wanted." We don't have a radar that goes off when a girlfriend-to-be passes by. We might feel an instant, undeniable attraction to a friend, or we may have seen her a hundred times without ever even saying "hello" until one day we start talking and a friendship grows. However it starts, we are glad that our fates have brought us together, that we are given a true girlfriend.

Friendship Chemistry

There are times when we meet a friend, and we experience a moment of "Aha!" We instantly know that this girl has friend potential. *She*, we think to ourselves, *is someone we want to get to know.* We see her in the halls at school. We hear one of our other friends talking about this girl she just met. We plop down on the bus and check out our seat mate. And we like what we see. Something in us knows that we were just meant to be friends with this girl. And we think she might just like to get to know us, too.

The quality that attracts our attention doesn't have to be a major one. "I noticed Jane's eyebrows. They were plucked so perfectly," recalls Joanne. "And she had these cool pens. Those two things were enough to get my interest!" But while these characteristics can be superficial, such as her looks or clothes, other times we recognize a girl's deeper qualities that attract us to a potential friend.

We often look for people with certain characteristics to become our friends. Arielle's friend Caty's personality came through the first time Arielle noticed her. And Arielle was immediately intrigued, even though she was only five years old. "Our kindergarten teacher was trying to quiet us down. Caty stood up on a chair and hollered something like, 'Everybody be quiet!' to the class. This got my attention, all right! It told me she was very independent, and I respected that even at such a young age. In fact, she is still independent today, and I still have respect for her."

Gabriela recalls the initial time she saw Stephanie. "When I first saw Stephanie I liked her right off the bat. She had this kind of real confident, self-assured, cheerful attitude, which was so attractive to me. It made me feel as if we were already connected because I like to see myself that way as well. We were in an art class together, and I noticed how focused and independent she was. To me, she is definitely a model of a strong woman, and I love that in a friend." And Gabriela tells us how her initial impressions were accurate and have contributed to a long-lasting friendship. "When you are around Stephanie all the time, her confidence becomes contagious. Although I feel that I was already a confident person, being around Stephanie only increases the way I feel about myself. She shows her confidence through her independent nature, and also through her ability to organize and take the lead in many different situations."

Sometimes we notice people for a while and decide they are someone we'd like to get to know better. "Hannah caught my interest because of her sense of humor," says Jenny. " I had noticed how much she made other people laugh, and it wasn't because she was making fun of someone. She does great imitations of people, like teachers, famous people, her other friends. She repeats something they say in their exact voice and with their gestures. She doesn't do it behind people's backs, and even the person she imitates cracks up. It's like she does it in an affectionate way and draws you into her sense of humor. It got to the point where I would see her and think, 'Imitate *me*, imitate *me*,' so I'd know she noticed me."

 Jennifer's Connection Equation

$$\frac{Friendship}{Chemistry} = Smile + Energy + Sense\ of\ Humor$$

Often, we choose a friend who is the way we want to be. If we hang out with this friend, we will be like her. Her ways will rub off on us, and we can learn from her. This can be a positive experience, as Courtney discovered. "Rebecca is one of those people who has her act together. She always knew what to say, was on the honor roll, and even got the lead in the school play. Even though the teachers loved her, we didn't hate her for it. I thought if I could be her friend, I could learn to be confident like she was. I asked her to be my partner in drama class, where we had to make up a skit. I completely bombed my lines, and she covered for me and just blew it off like it was no big deal. We became friends, and I really have learned so much from just being around her. I'm more comfortable speaking up when I have something to say and not worrying about making a mistake."

Joy's friend Elaine embodies the qualities she wants for herself. "Elaine has this shine and passion. She is determined to succeed in theater as an actor, and she is a damn fine one, I might add. Her extreme love and devotion to that art is amazing. Seeing that in her makes me strive for the same thing." Britt tells us, "I look for friends who have high spirits, like my friend Nicole. There is no point in being friends with someone who is depressing. It will only bring you down. You know what they say—'misery loves company.'"

Whether we are intrigued by a physical characteristic like Joanne was or by a remarkable sense of self as sought by Arielle and Jenny, observing people is often the first step in long, fulfilling friendships with the young women who will be there to support us through it all. Or we may take a more proactive approach like Britt, Lacey, and Joy by surrounding ourselves with upbeat, positive people who will bring out the best in us. Although we can't force a friendship to happen, we can keep our eyes peeled. It may happen in an instant, but the friendship can last forever.

Just by Chance

Sometimes a friend comes along when we aren't even looking. We are thrown together by the fates, and the rest just happens by itself: we find common ground and become friends. Our mothers are friends, our last names start with the same letter so we sit next to each other in homeroom, our friends introduce us. We might not be expecting or looking for a new friend, but fate seems to have a different plan for us.

Katie Lou's and her friend Ames's mom encouraged their friendship from the time they were three years old. "My mom and Ames's mom were chatting at a 'meet the teachers day for preschool.' They introduced us to each other and continued to enroll us in the same dance classes and gifted child enrichment programs so we would always be able to see each other. And we recognized the underlying agenda: so they could see each other too."

Nikole also met her best friend, Brittany, through her mom. "I was riding my pink and yellow bike with the radio on it down the street while her mom was washing her car. She noticed that we had the exact same bike and asked how old I was. It turned out that we were only two months apart! She told me to wait while she went to get her daughter," Nikole laughs. "Too bad we got rid of the bikes; those were great bikes. But we didn't get rid of our friendship."

Jess met Kristin when they were on the playground and Kristin needed some advice. "We were sitting on the playground on the parallel bars. She asked me about a boy in my class who had been my boyfriend. He had made me cry when he broke up with me — mind you, this was in the third grade! Therefore, I told her not to like him because he was mean. Kristin stayed away from him and we became best friends. By the way, I ended up dating that boy again this year. Yes, he has changed his ways. Isn't it crazy how things work out?"

 Top Five Random Ways We Meet
Our Friends

1. We sit near them in class—which leads to sharing pens, to being partners, to passing notes.

2. A mutual friend introduces us—and sometimes we become better friends with her than the mutual friend!

3. We live in the same neighborhood—but the bond turns out to be more than just convenience.

4. We are in the same club or group—shared interests get the conversation rolling.

5. Our parents are friends—so we would be forced to be anyway.

Becoming partners in class can lead to becoming friends in real life. Joanne remembers how she and Kim first got to know each other better. "We both didn't have partners for a science lab—which involved dissecting frogs—and so that's where our friendship started. We were extremely grossed out by the whole idea of taking apart a frog's body, especially in the class period right before lunch. I remember that neither one of us wanted to touch the frog, but in the end Kim had her fingers on it the most. A group next to us started throwing around frog parts, and one part landed on Kim's desk. It was extremely gross but very fun. In our yearbook, she wrote to me, 'I hope we're in class together next year—and if we are, it better be science.'"

"I think my teacher was setting us up to be friends on purpose," recalls Ashley about the first time she met her friend Steph. "She told us to choose partners in class for a speech and suddenly she announced, 'Steph, you and Ashley can be partners.' We had to work together every afternoon for a week. It was an unlikely pairing because Steph was very outgoing and popular, while I was more studious and shy. For the speech it worked really well. I helped Steph research and organize, and she helped me find my voice so I could present the speech to the class. We started passing notes back and forth to each other that started out serious but turned to teasing. Like I would write, "Did you find the information online?" but then she would draw a picture of me standing in front of the class, shaking and letting out a huge burp. After we gave such a good speech, we couldn't give each other up. And a year later we are still great friends and note-passers."

A statement made in passing led Joy to find her girlfriend Elaine. "A friend of mine mentioned that I reminded her of her friend Elaine. At the time, I was in what could be considered an abusive friendship, and I felt I needed to make friends outside of her and her circle. So I told her to give me her number, and I would see what it was about this Elaine that made my friend think of me. I had no clue who this chick was, what she liked, anything. We made pointless small talk, and I kind of thought she wasn't interested in being my friend at all. After a bit, she said she needed to go and that was the end of the conversation.

"Six months later, I called her again on a whim. I had kept her number written on my bookcase by my phone. I was still in the 'abusive friendship' (and I would be until Elaine convinced me of how unhealthy it was), and I called her again to try and prove to her that I had other friends besides her. It was a Saturday night and I asked her if she wanted to go to the movies. We had never met in person, and we had only talked once on the phone. But she said yes. I actually haven't thought of this day in a long time, and now that I'm recalling it, I can smell the barely spring air. I can clearly see her pulling up in her little green Beetle and stepping out, dressed in one of the hippie shirts she liked to wear then and jeans. I walked out onto my porch, and she called from the driveway, 'Hey,' almost like we'd met before.

"That night, we went to the movies and catastrophe struck. It was the moment I realized I wanted to be friends with her and the moment, I think, we bonded. I went into the movie before her, and when she didn't come in after a while, I went outside the theater to find her. She lost her money and couldn't get into the movie, then she couldn't get in touch with her parents, and *then* she locked her keys in her car. She was standing at the pay phone crying, leaving a message on her parents' voice mail. I gave her a hug, and then we walked over to her car to discover the keys sitting on the seat. I waited with her as a woman went and got a coat hanger and then unlocked her car. We missed more than half of the movie, but I didn't care. After the mishaps at the movie theater, we joked around and talked like we had known each other for a while. We really had bonded. After that day, we started hanging out every day—after school, on weekends, etc. And it's been that way for three years."

"It was impossible not to be friends with Amihan," laughs Jessica. "We went to the same school, played all the same sports, and her dad was the coach of our softball team. So I had to be her friend. Plus, she was just too nice."

Whether we were set up to be friends, like Katie Lou and Nikole, or tossed together by circumstances, like Ashley and Jessica, the connection can be as strong as if we had searched and searched for the perfect friend.

A Rocky Start

Sometimes, we make a friend who is so unexpected she never would have made our Top 100 Potential Friends List. We often have a vision in our mind of the type of person with whom we are friends. And then someone comes along and shatters that illusion and becomes a girl-friend.

Such was Ami's experience. "When I met Kat, my first thought was: total loudmouth, insane, boy-crazy wacko! She was just this girl who ended up sitting next to me when the seating chart changed in science class. I didn't plan to have anything to do with her, and the feeling was mutual. Her first thoughts about me were that I was a serious, quiet, smart girl—totally not her type. She's boy crazy, where I'm nature crazy. She's really into music, where I know nothing about music. I horseback ride well, and she's afraid of horses! That was last year, until we found out how much we had in common and could talk about. And both of us found science boring. But different as we are, we always enjoy hanging out and sparring with each other and laughing at each other. And we're always there for the other."

Opposites can attract in our friendships. We are quiet; our friend doesn't shut up. Our bedroom walls are plastered with pictures of guy bands; she doesn't know one group from another. But our different personalities can complement each other. After all, if your friend talks nonstop, who better than a good listener to be her best friend? And when we spend five straight hours writing love letters to each of the guys in 98 Degrees, we need someone to drag us out of our room and take us Rollerblading.

"Kate and I are entirely different!" Allison tells us. "She's completely antisocial; I'm a party girl. She's a sophomore; I'm a senior. She's not really school involved, and I'm involved in tons of things. Also, Kate's not very girly, she wears dark colors, and to see her in a skirt is a big deal. But I'm into skirts and the girlish stuff. I'm sporty; she's more poetry."

"I can't even think of what Jessica and I do have in common," laughs Elizabeth. "She likes to wear dresses and skirts; I am shorts and jeans. She is makeup and hair; I am no makeup and 'who cares about hair'? She likes to dance; I personally won't do that in public. But for some reason, we click."

Alisa and her two best friends are very different, but the differences bring balance to their friendship. "Meghan is very boisterous and outgoing. Tiffany seems the typical dingy chick, although she is very smart. I am smart and kind of shy. Tiffany doesn't have a boyfriend, Meghan does but he treats her like gold. I have a boyfriend too, but it's not the best relationship because I let people push me around. They are doing a good job of talking me into breaking up with him. When the three of us are together, we kind of fill in for each others' flaws. If one of us can't do it then at least one of the others can."

"Krista was loud spoken and I wasn't," Angel recalls. "I was kind of amazed by her. She would hold these burping contests in the school cafeteria and win them. I didn't like to burp; I couldn't make myself burp if my life depended on it."

We can't count on our first impressions. Our judgment can be way off, as Christine told us. "When Lizzie was new at my school, I thought she was a know-it-all. We were doing Africa, and her school had done Africa last year so she was always giving the answers. But my friends' mothers were friends with her mother, and their mothers told them to be nice to her. So my friends made me sit with her at lunch and everything. And as I got to know her I realized my impression of her was wrong. And now we are really good friends."

Charlotte had a negative impression of Allie when Charlotte was the new girl at school. "There was a popular group at my school and Allie was in it. I just assumed she was stuck up. But we were playing basketball one day, and she asked me about my bracelet. I wear the name of my horse, Sweet on Joe, on a band on my wrist. It turned out she rides horses too. And when we got to know each other, we became best, incredibly close, friends."

Sometimes a girl seems out of reach as a friend. Jessica remembers thinking that Lisa was out of her league. "She was always a step ahead of me. She was smarter, all the guys were in love with her, and she seemed perfect. Later, I found out that all along she had been admiring me because I was very athletic and she wasn't at all."

Cecily's Top Five List of What NOT to Say to a Potential Girlfriend

1. "I can't believe you just did that. How are you ever going to show your face in school again?"
2. "Your boyfriend is a total hottie. I want him."
3. "Did you do that to your hair on purpose?"
4. "When you guys break up, let me know. I'll pick up the pieces."
5. "You know, I don't really like you, but since your brother is gorgeous, I'll keep on coming over to your house."

It's a good thing Cecily's soon-to-be friend didn't use first impressions to rule out their friendship! "I was at karate one day, and I was close to crying because I wasn't getting the move correctly. I had a runny nose, and it kept dripping. I wiped my nose on my arm and looked up, and this girl Kana was looking at me. She didn't say anything or give me the grossed-out look I am sure I deserved. I knew then I could trust her to not laugh at me. I was right, too!"

Moon remembers meeting her friend Christie on vacation. "The hot Florida sun that my New Jersey-born self had never experienced caused me to retire early from running around the water parks. I returned to my room to take a cold bath in a desperate attempt to lower the heat of my burning body. My unnaturally pale skin was forming dark pink patches, turning into a very severe case of sun poisoning.

"I popped my headphones over my ears and started listening to some happy techno in an attempt to bring my miserable, painful mood up a few notches. I waited for the elevator to bring me to the first-floor food court. I stepped into it and stood among a family with a young child staring at my bubbled burned skin. The mother turned my pain into a lesson for her daughter. I felt my face getting redder with embarrassment, knowing that I had, in fact, forgotten to put on enough sunscreen. The rest of the ride down seemed to last forever. Finally getting off, I turned my music back up and began walking to the beat and not paying attention. A girl wearing an ultra-trendy shirt and shorts ran into me, sending me falling to the ground, landing on my blistered back. With the blisters ripped open and oozing, I started crying with frustration and pain. We both felt rather bad about our stupid run-in. We went to the bathroom, and she helped clean me up. Then we treated each other to lunch. Over the two or so hours we talked, we learned a lot about each other, and we both learned that the other wasn't the stereotype we thought we were. She thought I was a raver bitch type (my angry rant when I fell didn't help); I thought she was an obnoxious trendy snob. We ended up going to Epcot together and getting rather close. My painful run-in brought about two things: patience, and the knowledge that not every trendy person is a bitch."

Friendships don't always start out smoothly. We might have disliked or even "hated" someone who later became a girlfriend.

Char told how everyone knew she and Leah were meant to be friends—everyone except Char and Leah. "Leah is now one of my best friends, but I used to hate her. For four years I couldn't stand her, and at one point I thought I would leave our school just to get away from her. We finally came to the decision just to stay away from each other. Our parents said one day we would be best friends and look back at this and laugh. We only rolled our eyes and stormed off. But eventually, we started a friendship. It has grown and now we are stronger than ever."

Melissa and her now-friend Jacqui described themselves as archenemies. " When I met Jacqui we absolutely hated each other for the longest time. We always fought and pulled each other's hair. We had gotten to the point where our parents and teachers were sick of us fighting. When we were in fourth grade, we were in the same class and got stuck sitting next to each other. We eventually started talking and realized that the other wasn't as bad as we had thought. We ended up being the best of friends."

Perhaps we appreciate these friendships that begin with a rocky start even more, in a way, since we overcame hurdles and first impressions and found out that what we have in common is far greater than what separates us.

Reaching Out

It isn't always easy to make a new friend. "What if she doesn't want to be friends with me?" we wonder. "What if I wind up humiliated for my efforts? Is it easier *not* to make the effort?" But we learn that the potential rewards far outweigh the odds of rejection.

Some people seem to effortlessly find new friends. Zoe is one of those girls who is comfortable meeting new people. She is open to the possibility of a new friend wherever she goes. "How do I meet my friends? I just talk to everyone everywhere: at school, at parties, in diners, or wherever. It's easy to make friends anywhere if you just talk to people, joke around, jump into conversations."

Cecily puts strangers at ease with her friendly, straightforward attitude. Her outgoing nature also allows her to meet many friends. "I am the one who usually initiates friendships. I am a very open and outgoing person. When

I see someone who looks like they'd be friends with me, I watch them for a while to see how they act. Do they smile and laugh? Are they kind to others? Are they too image conscious? If I like them, I will go up and say something like, 'Hi! My name is Cecily. What's yours?' and then ask the usual questions about age, etc. I try to comment on something out of the ordinary because that usually makes them feel more comfortable. Sometimes that person and I don't become friends, but I will at least know how old she is and stuff (always good to know, I think). Sometimes, other girls who I didn't see will come up to me and say 'hi.' I am always glad when this happens because, other than being easier on me, I always make new friends."

Britt finds that sharing a laugh is the best way to make a new friend. She insightfully tells us, "Laughter is the best way to break the ice. If eyes are the window to the soul, a smile is the front door."

There are plenty of ways we can open our heart to new friends, even if we are shy, introverted, or downright tongue-tied. Katie Lou was feeling shy but then noticed that a girl in her class seemed to feel equally out of place, so she approached her. "My physics class was made up primarily of annoying, ditzy, popular girls and their male equivalents. Neither of us had any friends in there, and we were both sitting alone looking very nerdy and unpopular. I figured, why shouldn't we at least team up and be alone together? So one day I just took the empty seat next to her and started talking to her. I found out we have a lot in common. We are both really smart, but not exactly Science People. We were bored and didn't quite get it so we spent our time making up dumb jokes, having each other read our writing, and basically avoiding doing anything intellectual. Not the best utilization of class time, but at least we got to be really good friends!"

Melissa's outgoing friend Jessica chose her as a friend, and there was no mistaking that *she* wanted to be friends with *Melissa*. "My oldest friend is one of the hundreds of Jessicas that I know. The teacher was talking, and we were all sitting together on the rug on the floor. Out of the corner of my eye, I saw someone sliding over to me. Then I felt a tap on the shoulder, and a girl asked me straight out, 'Do you want to be my friend?' and I said 'Yes,' and she was the first friend I made at that school. And we're still friends!"

Being shy sometimes is misconstrued by others. We want to be friendly, but our clammy hands and racing hearts might make it difficult for us to be outgoing. "It's hard for me to make friends," shares Kaia. "It's this fear that I am different and I will automatically be rejected or used. I made the friends I am with today by going into school one day really upset, and I suppose I just looked like I needed to talk to someone. A couple of the girls had thought I was an uptight snob until they saw me that way. They asked me if I was OK, and then we found we all felt messed up about things."

Melissa also believes her shyness gives people a negative first impression. "I am a shy person at first, and it takes a lot to get me to warm up to someone. Most people don't even try to talk to me because they think I am stuck up."

Trinity's friend Kim used humor to help her find her voice and overcome her shyness. "She was tired of me hanging back when she wanted to go out and socialize. She showed me how painful shy can be by pretending to be extremely shy when we went out and forcing me to hide with her until I was at the point of going up to people. She gave me a wake-up call. After that, we started playing games so I would be confident using my voice. Like, she would say a vulgar word, like penis, and make me say it. Then she would say it louder, and then I'd have to go louder, until we're both so determined to win we're screaming *peeeeeennniiisss!*"

Janessa recognized that her shyness got in the way of making true connections to new people. "I used to be extremely shy, but I have gotten over that. I learned not to worry about what people think of you. Just go up, introduce yourself, smile, and be yourself. It works!"

Laura was in the same boat. "I used to be the shiest person you could have ever met. I was always scared to make new friends for fear they wouldn't like the way I acted. This year was a major turnaround for me. I wasn't gonna let what other people thought of me bother me anymore. I started to go out and act myself, and eventually new people started talking to me. I even got myself a boyfriend who I could act normal around and didn't have to put on a play with. He liked me for me, and I realized that maybe everyone else would too. So I kept on being myself and started to make new friends left and right. In one school year, I made many new friends. I want people to like the real me. And if they don't like the real person, they don't deserve to be my friend."

Jessica had a tough time meeting friends when she first became homeschooled, but she overcame her shyness and took the initiative. "My first year of homeschooling, I was in fifth grade and feeling lonely and new to everything. My mom got me involved in all kinds of activities and field trips with our local homeschooling group so I could meet other homeschoolers. There were a few kids my age who I wanted to try and get to know, but at the time they seemed unfriendly and uninterested. This upset me, and I got really ly depressed feeling that I didn't belong in school, but I didn't have any friends while I was homeschooling. So for a while I just kept to myself, even though I was lonely.

"Over the years I continued to see these kids at different homeschoolers events, but we never really talked. None of us made any effort. Then two years ago, I decided I wanted to make more of an effort. I wanted to have friends I could relate to. My mom started talking with the kids' parents, and they planned some activities for us so we could get to know each other. At these activities I think we all just came out of our shells and started talking more. Maybe they just needed someone to take the initiative. We continued talking and hanging out together, and before we knew it we had formed our own 'older homeschoolers group.' Now we're all best friends."

Some of us are naturally friend magnets, like Zoe and Cecily. Sometimes it's as easy as laughing or simply asking someone, and voilà, you have a friend. For others, like Moon, Melissa, Trinity, and Janessa, it takes a while longer. But we learn that if we open the door a crack, a true friend is just outside, waiting to come in.

 Five Things to Do to Get a Conversation Started with a Potential Girlfriend

1. Compliment her on something she says, does, or wears.

2. Ask her a question about homework or school.

3. Sit across the aisle from her on the bus and lean over to ask a question. If you sit next to her, you might be taking someone else's usual spot and look too pushy.

4. Pass her a note in class about something that isn't personal. If she doesn't respond, you know she doesn't want to get to know you, but at least the rejection isn't to your face.

5. Say "hi!"

Join the Club

When we are involved in activities outside of school, we have a new realm in which we expand our world of friends. We have the opportunity to meet people in different grades, different schools, and different cliques. We make many new friends through extracurricular activities such as drama, youth groups, and dance. We share hobbies with friends that include music, art, dance, writing, reading, photography, cooking, and animals.

Sydney didn't think any of the people in her extracurricular activity would become her friends, but she soon discovered otherwise. "I met Megan because we were in marching band together. Well, she was in the band, and I was labeled a 'band aide.' I didn't think that anybody in the band would accept me because I didn't actually make it into the band by playing an instrument. I was just there to help them out. Megan and I began to hang out, and we instantly clicked."

While we might become involved in activities because they spark our interest or because we have a special talent, the activities often become subordinate to bonding with a friend. When Jennifer met Embry, they were both photography novices. "While our interest in photography waned rather quickly, our friendship didn't. While I enjoyed taking pictures, the teacher's endless droning about shutter speed and light threatened to turn me off to cameras permanently. But Embry was my partner, and I found her interesting enough to suffer through the club."

Allison and Kate became quick allies and then quick friends while in theater together. "We were building a set with papier-mâché, and everyone building the set got into this *huge* war, throwing the papier-mâché *everywhere*. Kate and I put our backs to each other and fought together against everyone else. I had invited some of the cast to my house afterward and told her to stop by. When I gave her directions, it turned out she only lives two blocks from me. So we're always running over to each other's house now."

Churches, synagogues, and other houses of worship were other places girls responded that they found their girlfriends. Kim and her friend Brandi enjoy attending church together. "We are both Catholic, and we went to the same Catholic school for eight years. We strongly believe in our faith in God. Going to church together brings us closer with God as well as each other. We talk about how much we appreciate what God has done for us."

"My friends and I have shared experiences such as our Bar and Bat Mizvahs together," says Char. "We have studied Torah together and done spiritual prayers together. We can come together as Jewish people and feel accepted among ourselves. Exploring our spiritual selves brings us together, closer, as friends."

Rosemary has found true friendship among members of her youth group at her church. "I am privileged to belong to a group of truly beautiful people at church. Our group meets every Sunday while our parents attend the regular church service. We are so lucky to be a part of this group. When we are there, we know that everyone around us truly appreciates us and can be trusted. Every person is honestly an angel. It's amazing. We come together as a support group to talk about God and our own divinity. We meditate and pray. And we have fun! This group has brought me together with my platonic soul mate and with the people I love most in the world."

A friend who shares one of our passions is a real treasure. When we love something, sharing that love with another person can create an intense understanding between the two of us.

Joy and Elaine share a passion for self-expression and creative inspiration. "My passion is writing, and Elaine and I were in a writer's group together. Elaine was the first person to ever take my love of writing seriously, to ever say that I could do something with it. She was the first person I ever let read my stuff. She knows how important it is to me, when others can't understand it. One time, we went to a concert with friends, and as the concert was winding down, I got a spark of inspiration. I took out this little notebook I had and started writing. As I was writing, I heard one of her friends ask her what I was doing. She said, 'She's writing. She really gets into her writing.' It's hard to describe how that made me feel, the fact that she *knew* what was going on in my head. The way she said it, it was like, 'Duh! Don't you know *Joy?*' It was important to me to know she knew me that well. I also write for her. Kurt Vonnegut, my absolute favorite writer, once wrote that there are eight rules to creative writing. Rule number seven is to write for one person. I had never really thought about it before I read that. I know I write for her. Not for her approval, but just . . . for her. Usually I write my poetry like I'm talking to her. Even though it may not be about her or anything to do with her, it comes easier when I think about talking to her."

 How Lindsay and Fanny Share a Passion for Fashion

1. We've designed a clothing line together.

2. We're always reviewing each other's ideas and making suggestions for improvement.

3. We read the fashion mags together for ideas.

4. We came up with our future store name together: Sweet Stuff. Keep an eye out for it!

5. We share a goal: by age sixteen we will be fashion divas.

Allie and Charlotte say that their love of horses is a common bond in their friendship. "We have both ridden horses since we were young. We met because she noticed my bracelet with my horse's name on it," says Charlotte. "This interest has brought us together," agrees Allie, "because we are always talking about horses. Not everyone would be interested, but we are passionate."

We find pleasure in music, a thrill in being onstage, or serenity exploring our spirituality and religion. And whether we have a fleeting interest like Jennifer, or a true passion like Joy, we find that a common activity can be the deliciously fateful link that brings us a new soul mate.

On the Same Team

Girls who play sports are more likely than other girls to have higher self-esteem, better body image, and lower stress levels, and to avoid harmful behaviors such as smoking and using drugs. Of course the physical activity has a lot to do with that, but the deep bonds we form with teammates as we experience victory and defeat make us stronger and more confident. And stronger and more confident girls make better friends. Being teammates means spending a good deal of time together. Many tight friendships are formed as teammates experience the greatest of wins and the worst of defeats together.

Jenny discovered her enjoyment of a sport when a friend talked her into it. "I started playing basketball because my friend's dad was coaching the team. She asked me to play with her. I wasn't too sure, but I said OK and ended up liking it. We became really close from playing. The team was a combination of girls from different grades, so we all got to know new people as well."

Elizabeth tells how sports have helped her friends bond tightly. "I play a lot of sports, and while rowing crew, as a team we must have spent close to twenty-four hours a week just practicing together. Through that we all became very close and would go out to lunch or see movies as a team. Working that hard with a group of people really brings you close together. They are the ones that see you out of breath and exhausted and cranky and who can empathize with your pain. Some of the best friends I've made have been through sports."

Having a friend on our team is wonderful in so many ways: we have someone to chat with in the locker room; we celebrate our victories together; we cry at defeats and pull together to face our opponents. It's also great to have a friend to help us when we just can't seem to get it right.

Brittanie recalls how she met her friend Sam on the swim team. "My friend Sam and I met when she started swimming two years ago. She was a younger swimmer and I was older. Our coach put us into little groups so that us older kids could help out with the younger kids. Sam was put into my group. I can remember our coach telling her to keep her knees together when she was swimming breaststroke and me, being sick minded, yelling, "That's a good abstinence lesson, Sam!" We both broke out into hysterics, and now she's one of my best friends. Of course I still ended up with dips as a punishment, even if our coach secretly thought it was hilarious, because some parents were sitting there. It was funny though. It was the joke of the season." Brittanie continues to describe her swim team as her extended family. "Along with Sam, my good friend Sarah also swims with me. We have all been swimming together since we were six. What is so great is that everyone on the team gets along, and we never seem to have any fights. It's constant competition but in a good way. Like, if I win it's great and if you win that's great, too. You make such good friends. You can lose and still be excited over the other person's win. We all support each other. It seems like I see the girls on the team every waking moment. I don't know what I would do without them."

Cecily tells us, "One place I have met good friends is at karate class. When you are attacking and then throwing each other on the ground, you get to know each other rather quickly! The lower ranks of students have their group as do the higher-ranking students. The nice thing about the class, however, is that the higher belts are assigned to help the lower belts; therefore, everyone mingles, and we are all nice to each other."

Laura and her friend Erin spent many years as teammates on the cheerleading squad. "Erin and I have been cheering together for seven years, and we have always had the best of times together. We have so many memories from all those times. It's different this year, though, because she made the squad and I didn't. I miss it so much, and when I didn't make it, she helped me through it. She was there for me through the whole thing. She didn't care that she made it; she was just making sure I was OK and that I was strong and that I could get through it and shouldn't give up."

 Top Five Ways to Support Your Sporty Girlfriend

1. Attend her games even if she spends most of the time warming the bench.

2. Don't give her a hard time if she has spent less time with you because she needs to practice or play.

3. Attend one of her away games and cheer louder than their home audience.

4. Give a "you-go girl" card after an important game.

5. Encourage each other, even if you are on opposing teams.

Lessons of friendships come through sports. Susan Wilson, author of *Sports Her Way: Motivating Girls to Start and Stay with Sports*, wrote: "Sports provided me with the opportunity to meet hundreds of new people. Whether I was competing against other schools as an athlete, instructing children in my gymnastics classes, attending workshops as a coach, or traveling internationally to athletic events, I have had a chance to share ideas with, struggle with, and be excited about accomplishments great and small with all kinds of people, at all levels of experience."[2]

Clique, Clique

We hang in groups, in packs, in crews. We might be a member of one group, and everyone knows we are part of this certain gang of friends. The group might be established and exclusive, where gaining admittance is hard and you are dropped if you don't conform. Or we might not be part of one clique, but be in different groups at different times. The group we always sit with at lunch is different from the group we hang out with on Saturday night and the group we compete with at soccer. Or we might move along by ourselves, intermingling with different groups or with no groups at all.

"When I was a kid, my friends Josie and Shawn made up the 'Cool Club,'" Ivy says. "And only cool kids were allowed in it. It's almost scary how serious we were. We had T-shirts and everything. Now my friends and I are in our own little club. We don't have T-shirts, but we still operate by exclusion. In its own way, perhaps this is even more scary."

Most schools consist of groups that are identified by labels. Trinity describes the different groups in her school. "We've got the preps, the jocks and cheerleaders, the trendy people, and the ravers, skaters, goths, freaks, and druggies." At Kim's school, she says the cliques are the athletes, popular, nerds, cool nerds, brains, and the wannabe populars. The athletes are the ones who are in sports and party all weekend. The popular ones are the ones who everyone thinks are snobs because they are so sarcastic with each other. The nerds are the ones who are quiet and shy. The cool nerds are the ones who everyone likes but who are friends with the nerds. The brains are the really smart ones. The wannabe populars are the ones who think they're all that and a bag of chips. There are more people in this clique than in any other one. The caste system at Ami's school includes "the preppies/cheerleaders, the jocks who hang with them, punkers and rockers, goody-goodys, and the geeks, who study, study, study and we all know will someday be millionaires, but we just can't befriend them despite that knowledge."

Hanging out in a group can make us feel included, like we know where we belong. When our group is made of true friends, we feel protected and comfortable. Janessa feels that she is safe when she is with her group of friends. "In my opinion, cliques are not that bad. They give you a sense of security, like you know you have someone or somewhere to go to. Some people consider cliques bad because most people in the popular group won't talk to unpopular people, and it makes people feel bad about themselves. I am considered to be in the popular group in my school. But even though I am in that group, I talk to everyone that I know, whether they are shy, unpopular, or whatever."

Echo believes that cliques are a natural part of life. "Most of us are part of some group or another. Being in a clique isn't necessarily a bad thing, as long as it doesn't exclude other people."

But for others of us, the word clique only brings up negative thoughts. A clique is defined as a small group of exclusive friends or associates. Even the definition points out that all girls in a clique might not be friends, they just "associate"! Allison tells us her views on cliques. "To me, a clique is a bad thing. When I hear the word *clique*, I think of the cheerleaders that go around and make fun of those they don't approve of." Stephanie makes a point: "I tend to think that cliques are bad to be in, just because sometimes people rely on each other too much. It's a disturbing thought, but sometimes you don't know who will be there till the end and who will turn on you in a second. That's why you shouldn't limit yourself to a single clique of people; you should try to make new friends." Jilli's group of friends is flexible. "We aren't a distinct group, like a clique. Instead, there's a big group of people that also hang out with many different people. There are times I need to talk or just simply be around somebody, and this way I can almost always have someone there when everyone else isn't available."

Some cliques are made of external forces. Girls are grouped off based on who they've always hung out with, what they wear, the guys they date.

Many girls say there are downsides to being in the popular group. Annabel feels this way: "At my school, the girls in the popular clique aren't really genuinely liked. They are admired, copied, and feared, but not necessarily liked. If the popular group in my school was made up of the nicest, friendliest girls then it might be a group I'd like to hang with myself. But it's not, so I am happier with my own true crew."

Laura describes what she sees: "I don't know about other schools, but at my school, the popular group just doesn't have much fun. They act all serious and walk around like they are better then everyone else when we all really know they aren't. No one person is better than another. I had my choice to be in the popular clique. My best friend introduced me to a lot of the girls, and we hung out for a while. But I decided I wasn't having any fun. So I left and made new friends, which I think was the best move of my life. So what if we aren't the most popular girls in school? It doesn't matter to us. We know we can trust each other. The girls in the popular clique are constantly fighting. Their idea of fun is to go out on weekends and get drunk. You don't need alcohol or drugs to have a good time. My friends and I have a great time without it."

We all know which cliques are which by being around one another, but sometimes different cliques are equally apparent to the outsider. Patricia describes how her high school had different levels of popularity at the lunch table. "When I went to high school my class had three different lunch tables. We had the popular table. Those were the people who wore like Gap, Abercrombie, and stuff like that. Then you had my table where just anyone who wanted to sit with us could. And then you had the loser table. Those were the people who no one seemed to like. I never thought that I would be friends with someone from the popular table, but now I am really good friends with one of them. And also I never thought that I would become friends with anyone from the loser table, but now that I have got to know different people, I'm now friends with a lot of people that I never thought I would be friends with."

Jessica R. was bothered by the fact that her friends separated themselves into distinct groups, so she took a risk and mixed up her friends from different groups. "About a year ago, I wanted to have a Halloween party and invite my homeschooled and schooled friends. I really wanted the two groups to meet, but I was worried that they wouldn't get along. Everyone has their own ideas and has heard stories that homeschoolers are 'antisocial nerds' or that school kids are 'gossipy and shallow.' I didn't want any of this to come out at the party. I wanted all stereotypes erased. In the beginning of the party, everyone was quiet. People were grouping off, and I wondered if I had made a mistake trying to bring people together. But as people relaxed more, they began to talk and I was relieved to see that, by the end, everyone was getting along and having fun. Later on, everyone had good things to say about each other, and they were very happy that I introduced them. They've all kept in touch by e-mail, and there's no more weird silence at other parties."

Girlfriends know that what group you are in does not signify who you are. Being a member of a group can be a positive or a negative, but it is up to you to know the difference. What group we are in can be a way of forming our identity. It can help you find your niche, a place you feel safe and welcome. But sometimes being in a group can be the easy way out. It might seem easier to be known as a cheerleader and just act like the rest of the cheerleaders than to really explore who you are and what you really want to be.

Laura has this advice about being in the popular clique: "The best advice I could give is to not even waste your time trying to be in the popular group. If you are in it and you are popular because you are nice to people, then great, fine, enjoy it. If you are not in it or the so-called popular group is exclusive, then it's not worth it. You might look at the girls who are in that clique and wish to be exactly like them, but on the inside those girls might be screaming to get out. Be with people who appreciate you, not your social status." Sydney agrees. "Actually, one of my very best friends is always wishing to be popular, at least more popular than she is. She doesn't realize that people *do* like her. I told her that as long as *she* loved who she was and was trying to be exactly what *she* wanted to be, then that is the only thing that mattered. You shouldn't worry about what people think about you because everyone has different opinions; work on loving yourself." Janessa sums it up:"No matter what group you are in, or even if you aren't in a group, be happy about it. Be proud of yourself and your accomplishments, and don't let anyone tell you differently."

Popularity

Being popular is what all teenagers strive for, right? If you are popular, it means you have the closest and best friends and the most fun, right? Not. Being popular may be a goal for some teenagers, but it doesn't automatically lead to having true girlfriends. So which is better, being popular or having a few close girlfriends?

"A few close friends! Definitely!" says Mia. "Popularity can come and go, but your true friends stick with you. I am actually in the so-called popular group at school, but I am closer to some girls than others. If you asked me which I would rather have taken away from me, my popularity or those couple of friends, I would choose just to have those couple of friends without a doubt."

Alisa agrees. "I think it is better to have a few close friends because that way you can always rely on them to be there, and you don't have to worry about what they think of you. You can just be yourself."

Despite the fact that the popular group tends to have the most wanna-bes, its members are not always the nicest people or even really enjoy their clique-mates. Bowing down to the goddesses of the In Clique has its price. Rebecca is in the popular group at school. "It's good to not be *so-o-o-o* popular because then you always have to live up to everyone's expectations and do what people expect you to. You should have as many friends as you want, but you shouldn't have to feel like you have to impress them all the time." Sydney tells us, "I really do believe there is a downside to being in the popular clique at my school because on all occasions I have seen they're just not very nice people. I myself am not very popular, but I try to make friends with everyone, not just the popular people. When I moved here in the sixth grade, I was the very first person in the cafeteria on my first day of school. The next girl to walk in was very popular apparently. Not knowing this, I smiled at her only to have her look down her nose at me and walk away. I crawled into a hole and cried. That's what made me so shy. I try not to act like that toward people because I know how much it hurt me when she did that."

Jessica W.'s views on popularity have changed while growing older. "In middle school there were tons of different cliques. When I first got to middle school, I really wanted to be one of those popular girls. So I started talking to them and having lunch with them. Once I was friends with them, I discovered a lot of them were really rude people. I was in the popular group for about a year. When I left that group of friends I felt so good. The people were so mean to the dorky people. Then in seventh grade I hung out with people that I really had nothing in common with so I didn't really like them too much. In eighth grade I started to like my friends. They are the kind of people that you can have lots of fun with, and they won't make fun of you if you act different than other people. That is one thing that I hate, when people try to act like other people just because they want to be like them. Now I am in my freshman year of high school. It is so much better than middle school! Most of the people don't care about cliques. The popular kids and the regular kids just blend in. It isn't like in the movies where high school is so much worse than middle school. So you girls who are having a hard time fitting in, don't worry. It will get better. Also a lot of times those popular girls don't get as far in life as the others."

From the outside looking in, it can seem like girls in the popular group have it made. But Caroline had a revelation when she met Tanae. "In eighth grade, I ran into Tanae, one of the popular girls, in the girl's room when no one else was in there. Her makeup was all runny, and she looked like she had been crying. I didn't really know her well; I wasn't in any of the popular groups or anything. I asked her if she was OK, and she said, no, she wasn't and she didn't have any friends. I pointed out that she was really popular, and she said that didn't mean anything. She said the girls were so nasty to each other, and she felt like she couldn't show her true personality because they would make fun of her or kick her out of the group or something. It turns out they were all at a party over the weekend where there were these college guys and drugs, and she snuck out because she didn't want to be a part of that. But there was another party coming up that weekend, and she would be expected to go. She talked to me for so long we were late to next period. I felt bad for her. Her friends wouldn't listen and be supportive of her, and she felt she could only talk to someone who was practically a stranger. It made me feel thankful for my friends that were true, and I didn't really envy the popular girls as much as I used to after that. I don't think they have the best values, and it sounds like they don't even really like each other. I don't know what happened to Tanae after that. She never talked to me again. But I hope she found some friends who would be true to her."

Jessica shares how her classmates recognized what the true meaning of popularity ought to be. "Our junior class had a poll for the yearbook, where we voted for 'Best Athlete', 'Most Likely to Succeed,' and all that. I was the yearbook editor and in charge of counting votes. There was this one category where I think the winners surprised everybody. One was 'Most Popular.' The vote for the first one was really close, between these two girls Jamie and Willow. Jamie was the traditional popular girl. She was really pretty, had the best clothes, dated the coolest guy, and all that. She also was stuck up. Willow wasn't even in the popular clique. Two girls from the popular clique were on yearbook staff, and they were all riled up when we were counting the votes. They kept saying Jamie deserved it, Willow wasn't even popular. Then Emily, our photo editor, told them to be quiet, that maybe Willow wasn't in their clique, but she was the nicest, most helpful, and most genuine person in the whole school. Emily said she was glad so many students had decided to vote on popularity based on who was the best 'friend' and not just the leader of the popular clique. At that point, I was really rooting for

Willow even though I hadn't thought of it that way before and had voted for Jamie. When Willow won, I was really happy. I think it sent such a great message about what it really should mean to be popular."

 Jamie's Five Reasons It Is Better to Have a True Friend Than Be Popular

1. It's easier to lose popularity than a true friend.
2. Popularity expects perfection. True friends expect you.
3. True friends are more dependable than popularity.
4. Everyone has problems, but true friends are better at solving them than popularity.
5. Popularity can't make you soup when you're sick.

Alisa and Lindsay know that the pressure of being popular can be more difficult than it is worth. As Jessica shows us, the girl who is there for us, respects us, and treats us well is the true girlfriend to be admired, regardless of her status. It seems a far more worthwhile goal to spend your energy finding true friends than fighting to gain or keep the status of being popular.

Girl Friends vs. Guy Friends

We are friends with guys. They don't have to be boyfriends, just guys we love to hang with. We catch rides with them to school, sit with them at lunch, instant message them at night. But there is something special and unique about our friendships with our girlfriends that we just don't share with the boys. These differences can be minor, as Gabriela points out, "Guys won't sit around and polish their nails with me!" "I can't go shopping at Victoria Secret with guys; now that would be embarrassing," laughs Christine.

 ### Five Things We Do with Our Girl Friends That Our Guy Friends Hate to Do

1. Shop 'til we drop
2. Do makeovers
3. Talk on the phone for hours . . . and hours . . . and hours
4. Act goofy
5. Complain about PMS

Or the differences can run deeper.

Laura says, "The general consensus is that being around our female friends is a special experience. When I'm with my girlfriends, we can hang out and do whatever we want and act like crazy people, and we don't care what other people think of us. With guys it is not as open or relaxed."

Jessica thinks that the best thing about girlfriends is that they like to talk—and listen. "Guys are good in the way they always want to do stuff. They're a lot of fun to be with. But I've found that they don't listen as well as girls do. My girlfriends listen to my problems and then try to give me advice and tell me their opinion. Guys will either pretend to listen and care, or they'll just talk about themselves!" "It's really hard for a guy to open up to you, which can make it hard to open up to them," Paige tells us. "With girlfriends I am comfortable having a heart-to-heart talk. Girls are OK about crying around people, but guys have to defend their image and not cry and be all tough. Crying about things to your girlfriends can relieve a lot of stress."

Spending time with our girlfriends gives us a chance to really be ourselves. "I'll admit it," Melissa confesses, "I'm totally shy around guys, especially the ones I like. But with my girlfriends, it's different. Why? Because with girls, you don't have to try and impress them. You can just be yourself." Some of us just feel more comfortable wearing no makeup and skanky clothes, sitting around with the girls acting like dorks.

Jamie confesses, "It's really weird, but I can't eat in front of guy friends, even if I've never had any romantic interest in them. I suppose it's because I've never had guy friends as close as my girlfriends, so I feel more self-conscious. And then, the less people who see how messy an eater I can be, the better."

Flick says, "Girls know the same things you do, feel the same things you do. My friendships with guys are great, but it seems we always have different agendas. There are certain things they can't relate to with me." And one of those things guys can't relate to are all the physical changes that happen to us during our teenage years. "Cramps? Bloating? PMS? Can't talk to the guys about those!" adds Jia Li.

And with some of our guy friends, there can be a thought hovering on the back burner of our minds. Does he like me more than a friend? Do I like him more than a friend? Should I like him more than a friend? Why doesn't he like me more than a friend? The Attraction Tension looms in the distance of our friendships with guys. OK, let's admit it: that tension can be fun, but we also need to let down our hair, do extravagant beauty treatments, and have a true heart to heart . . . with just the girls.

BFF: Our Best Friends

"BFF—Best Friends Forever!" As the girl we share our secrets with, the girl we feel the closest to, and, let's face it, our favorite of all our friends, our best friend enjoys exalted status. When the feeling is mutual, best friends share a bond like no other.

"A best friend is a true friend," says Patricia. "What makes my best friend a true friend is that she is one person who I can relate to like none other. She is someone who knows everything about me—even things that I try to hide and keep anyone at all from knowing. She has just been there for me throughout everything that has gone on in my life. No matter what time it is, if I have a problem I can call her and she will be there for me. A lot of the time friendships are indescribable through words. I mean, if a person asked me to describe my friendship with my best friend, I could almost say that words cannot show how much we care about each other. Words have limits; actions do not."

"A best friend," says Allie, "is not necessarily a person that you have known since you were babies. In fact, a best friend hardly ever is that, mainly because people change as they grow older into a teenager. A true best friend is a person who has influenced you in so many ways that you know that you'll never forget them. They have, in a sense, scarred your life forever—in a good way, that is. The difference between a best friend and another friend is that, with a best friend, you can tell them anything and know that it's safe. You are able to come to a best friend with any of your problems as soon as they occur and leave with a solution. People like these are hard to find but, once found, they'll be with you forever."

Rosemary considers her best friend her soul mate. "I have a friend who seems like a sister or maybe even more. Kristin is honestly the most beautiful, caring, and truly compassionate young woman I have ever met. We met through the church youth group we are both a part of. I was just thirteen and she was seventeen. In spite of our age differences, we became very close. Now we are closer than close. We actually call each other platonic soul mates. I have been truly blessed with her presence in my life. I know that many girls dream of having a friendship like ours, and I am so lucky to have one. Kristin and I understand each other in a way that is hard to describe. She plays so many roles in my life. Everything that she gives to me, I give back to her. That's how our relationship stays so strong: we give of ourselves to one another.

Rosemary recognizes that having a best friend means having the faith that she is there when you need her. "If I ever need help or advice, I know I can call her at any time, day or night, and she'll be there for me. And if she ever needs anything, I'll be at her house in an instant or doing whatever I can to defend her against any strife. We greatly admire each other, and we live in awe of the enormity of the relationship that we share. I have never been as close to anyone as I am to her. I know that we'll be this close our whole lives, and if reincarnation is true then I know we've been friends in other lives, too. We were destined to meet, and our friendship will withstand many tests."

Best friend status can be extended to more than one friend or to a group of friends. "My best friends are the girls I *always* sit by, and they *always* save me a seat. I never question inviting them to a party or to my house. They are always around me, they always care about me. We laugh all the time, and we can joke around with each other because we know we really all love each other so much," says Char. Jess has a group of best friends who has stayed together through thick and thin. "We have seen each other through bad relationships, bad grades, and bad hair days. We've survived fights, jealousies, and petty differences. It sometimes amazes me when I think about it that I have these three friends to count on, and they can count on me."

 ## Five Ways to Sign Your Best Friend's Yearbook

1. "Love ya like a sister I never had!"
2. "Friends 'til the end"
3. "Best friends forever, sisters till eternity"
4. "FF&A"
5. "BFFE!"

The title "best friend" can be used and abused, and so-called best friends can come and go. But the close bonds that girls like Patricia, Rosemary, and Allie feel toward their best friend are holding strong and true. These friendships that have been solidified over time, through trust and shared experiences, are gifts that cannot be purchased at any price.

New Friends, Old Friends

Old friends are comfortable; we can count on them; we have a common history that provides stability and continuity. They have seen us through good times and bad. With new friends, we can start with a clean slate. We are free to present ourselves as we are becoming, not as we have been.

 Five Favorite Fictional Girlfriends

1. Sara Crewe and Becky (*The Little Princess*)
2. Anne and Diana (*Anne of Green Gables*)
3. The Members of the Baby-Sitter's Club (*Baby-Sitter's Club* series)
4. Meg, Jo, Amy, and Beth (*Little Women*)
5. Daria and Jane (*Daria*)

Jessica ponders the balance between old friends and new. She believes we have to make new friends to keep our life new and exciting, and we do this by meeting new people and trying new things. "The advantage of new friends is that your relationship is young, so you can just be silly and have fun. You can just talk about fun stuff, like movies, music, and guys, and in the beginning you don't have to worry about the serious stuff that comes along with old friendships. Sometimes, the serious stuff just gets too serious, and you need an escape, so that's when it's great to have new friends around.

"But then again, sometimes all I want to do is talk to my old friends. They know me and understand me and love me for who I am. Old friends can never be replaced. My friend Leigh, who I've known since we were in diapers, is a great person to talk to. We're always there for each other, giving advice, cheering each other up. We've been through some of that serious stuff, and it tested our friendship, but we resolved everything, and we're closer than ever now."

You might have heard the saying "Make new friends, but keep the old. One is silver and the other's gold." Ami knows this saying and takes it to heart. "I'm a Girl Scout and have been one since daisy, and I'm now a cadet. So I've known that saying forever; it's practically my motto! It means keeping your friends, even if they grow away from you, because friends are important, and try to bring your friends together, even if they're different, because you love them."

We love our old friends because they know where we are coming from, why we act the way we do, and exactly how to make us feel better when things just aren't going our way. But we love our new friends, too. We have a chance to reveal ourselves and show that we have faith in our new friends. We have the chance to meet someone who fills a certain empty space in our hearts that we never knew we had. And when we introduce our old friends to our new friends, we form an unbreakable circle of love.

Cherishing
Our Friends

One thing is clear: we appreciate our girlfriends. We are thankful for the simple acts of kindness as well as the grander gestures. Our girlfriends share clothes with us, they share laughs with us. They even share their most precious gift: their hearts. When we are going off track, we are grateful when their advice, caring, and compassionate help steer us back on the right road again. We are grateful that they accept us for who we are deep down inside. We all know how much girlfriends enrich our lives. The stories that follow remind us what a true girlfriend is all about.

In Sync

It is said that everyone has a twin in the world who is like them in appearance and personality. Some of us seem to not only find our double, but to become friends with them. Jordan and her best friend are often mistaken for sisters. "My friend Ashleigh, we're so much alike it's scary. We like the same things, we do the same things, and people say we even look alike!" Brooke tells us about ways she and her friend Kim are like each other. "Kim is also smart and does well in school. She also wears contacts and is in the same grade, goes to the same school, and lives in the same town. She has a younger brother in fifth grade and so do I, and our brothers are even friends too."

Jessica and her friend are so much alike they even share the same name! "My friend Jessica and I are constantly reading each other's minds. Countless times we'll say exactly what the other person was thinking or finish sentences for each other. Somehow, we're just very tuned into each other's minds. If I say to Jessica, 'I have to tell you something,' she'll ask if it's about such and such, and there's no way she could've known except if she read my mind! Whenever I call her, she always says she knew it was me on the phone before she picked up. Sometimes when she calls me, I'm thinking of her right before the phone rings.

"About four years ago, Jessica and I went to the same summer camp. We never talked. After that summer, my family moved into a house on this isolated road in a very small town, and we found out that Jessica and her sister lived right down the road from us! How coincidental is that? Jessica and I became friends and we found out that we have all these weird things in common."

 ## Top Five Ways the Jessica Best Friends Are Like Twins

1. We have the same first name.
2. We have the same last initial (we're both Jessica R's).
3. We both love *Buffy the Vampire Slayer*.
4. We both have brown hair and brown eyes.
5. We both love to swim and hate math.

Synchronicity, or coincidences between friends who are close, can be almost too eerie to be true. Alisa tells a story she says is hard to believe but, she says, is totally true. "I had a friend when I was ten, and one night I had a dream about a burglar coming into my room through my window and stepping on my face. I awoke at 5:55 A.M. and thought, 'My friend is knocking on wood right now,' since she is superstitious about nightmares. Then I realized that was a weird thought since it was my nightmare, not hers. At school that day, she told me how she had a dream about a burglar coming through my window and stepping on my face. And she woke up at 5:55 A.M. and knocked on wood. I couldn't believe the same thing happened to us! Of course when I told her she couldn't believe it."

Allison and her friend Kate have a connection that seems almost unreal even to them. "My friend Kate and I found out that, though we are entirely different, we can read each other's thoughts. She can say two words of a sentence, and I already know what she means, where she's going with it, and I can easily finish the sentence word for word. It drives people insane because we can sit there and talk about someone, with that person *in the room*, and they never know. Nobody knows what we mean but us. And it's because we only have to say a few words and it's already transmitted. I swear that sometimes she's even said what I was thinking without me saying a thing."

Marianna tells of a connection to Ella that seems psychic to her. "Ella and I communicate through our minds, rather than our mouths. Many times, we would hang out and the only thing she had to do is look at me, and I would know what she was thinking or was about to say. Sometimes, when we're on the phone and I don't tell her that 'something', she'll figure it out by herself. It's amazing how two friends could have such a connection, without even being near each other. I hope that many other people will find such a connection with their friends because it's just absolutely beautiful. It feels like you're sharing a part of your soul with the other person, and that's one really precious bond that would be wonderful for friends to share with each other."

Humor

A shared sense of humor creates a bond between two people that can leave others scratching their heads. "Elaine and I have the same sense of humor that other people, well, just don't share," Joy tells us. "There are certain things that we could say to each other in front of other people, and they'd just look at us going 'huh?' as we crack up. We also handle things the same way. When we have a crisis, a problem in our lives, when we're trying to get a date, when our waiter doesn't bring us the right order, we could be interchangeable." Olivia also knows how powerful laughter is in unifying friends. "My friend Roxana and I laugh at just about anything once we get going, and we have so many inside jokes we practically speak a different language."

Stephanie and her friends Alyssa and Lindsay actually did make up a different language. "We made up our own language so that we could talk to each other without our parents or my brother, Julian, knowing what we were saying. We made up a few lines and ran over to my house calling out these words 'Kamoep, Kamoep, oft zuis totavis?' which meant, 'Julian, Julian, where are you?' When we found him we said some things to him in our new language. He was so puzzled he had no idea why we were talking to him in what he probably thought was gibberish. It was hysterical. We were laughing so hard our faces were beet red. My parents took a picture of us laughing. It's such a great picture. You can tell we were laughing so hard we were almost crying."

Zoe and her friend have secret traditions they follow that are unbeknownst to anyone else. "My best friend and I have our own code. For example, we pinky swear. To us, it's the ultimate promise. We never break a pinky swear. *Never*. We also have a way of saying good-bye: I say 'denouement' (don't even ask me how to spell that) and she says 'enchanté,' but we say it very dramatically and with these weird accents."

Arielle's friends Kelly and Elissa have such compelling laughter that one small giggle can turn into a true laugh riot. "When one of them starts to laugh, it catches on. All of my friends, including myself, start laughing as well. Then it turns into giggle mania, and we, most likely, aren't able to remember what we'd started laughing at in the first place. Really, that's what usually starts me laughing— when they laugh first. For example, if Kelly's in a silly mood, she might look at me and I'll stare back, then she'll start laughing hysterically. Pretty soon I'm laughing too, and it spreads like the flu!" Alisa's friend Meghan always makes her laugh. "She is always singing and dancing and stuff, and she is always singing to Britney Spears songs and pretending like she is in the music videos—but she overdoes it and it is just hilarious. I guess you have to be there."

Allison and her friend Taylor share their humor with their friends. "My friend Taylor and I write parodies of all these fairy tales and things like that, basing the characters on our friends. Then we grab everyone else and make movies out of them! It's so much fun because we can't ever finish our lines because we're laughing so hard, so the movie is just us falling over laughing."

Sometimes when we are in a bad mood, humor can help us snap out of our funk. Jamie knows she can count on her friend Liz to kick her out of a bad mood. "When I'm sad, I talk to my friend Liz, and she helps me be mad and get it out of my system. Then she starts doing something crazy that she'd never do in public, like make up silly songs. Pretty soon I'm too busy laughing to even remember being upset." Christy cheered her friend up this way: "I was at Karrie's house, and she was pretty bummed about some things so I put on a song and got on her bed and started singing to her. I took her hand and got on my knees and was singing it to her. It made her laugh for the first time in a while."

If laughter is the best medicine, then our friends are writing the prescription. Being silly, telling (and creating!)

inside jokes, and even making up inside languages are all ways we keep each other laughing. Finding a person who shares our sense of humor enriches our lives and makes our days more fun. As Stephanie puts it, "Every time we have fun together, it's a way of bonding. Bonding doesn't always have to come from a long intimate conversation; having fun and laughing together can bring you just as close to someone as the best conversation in the world."

 Five Reasons to Share a Laugh with a Girlfriend

1. To cheer you up when you are bummed
2. To make you feel someone understands you, even when others don't get the joke
3. To help you see the lighter side of a bad experience
4. To create a memory
5. Simply for the fun of it

Being Ourselves

Our most cherished girlfriends are the ones with whom we can be ourselves. We can genuinely relax and enjoy each other's company and know that we are with someone who likes us simply for being us. We have a zit, a bad hair day, a bad mood day? No need to hide it from them. "The best thing about my friends," says Allison, "is they don't expect me to be something I'm not. They know who I am, and I can be myself around them without feeling self-conscious. I never go back after a conversation with one of my best friends and go, 'I hope that didn't sound stupid!' We've seen each other at our best and at our worst, but it doesn't change a thing."

Cecily doesn't feel the need to impress her friend Stella. "One of the things I like about my friend Stella is she doesn't place much emphasis on clothes and fashion. Sure, she likes to look good, but I don't have to worry about showing up at her house wearing my lime green shorts and her blabbing it to her friends at school the next day!"

Jessica recognizes that girlfriends are not there to judge you, but to enjoy you. "Most of my friends are very accepting, so if I do say or do something stupid, we'll just laugh it off because they know that everyone does stupid stuff. I feel comfortable with my friends because we know each other's flaws and differences. We try our best to accept, forgive, and not judge each other. If I always felt self-conscious around my friends or I thought I had to impress them, then they wouldn't be my friends. Friends shouldn't make you feel that way. I remember once, a while ago, I was sleeping over at my friend Randi's house. We hadn't known each other for very long and we were still getting to know each other, but I considered her one of my good friends. So that night, when we were getting changed for bed, I was totally surprised when Randi started taking off her clothes in front of me. I was kinda shocked, so I turned away, and she said, 'It's OK, Jess, we're both girls here.' I realized that she was totally comfortable around me, and that made me relax and feel more comfortable around her."

We're not the It Girl? We aren't the Poster Girl for Coolness? Doesn't matter to a girlfriend; she values you for the person you are and who you want to be. "I am very comfortable around my friends and don't feel pressured when I am with them," says Stephanie. "My friends and I don't judge each other for how 'cool' our clothes are. We choose not to drink, smoke, or experiment with drugs. My friends know that the way you look has nothing to do with what kind of a person you are. Although it's fun to talk about guys, none of us are currently in relationships. There will be plenty of time for dating, and right now I don't want to be tied down to having a steady boyfriend. I'm sure in the next few years a lot of what I just said will change slightly, but right now I just want to enjoy my friends."

Stephanie shares the qualities that make her girlfriends so precious to her. "My friends and I are not superficial; we are trustworthy, respectful, compassionate, playful, creative, and down-to-earth. Even though we have our disagreements, we resolve them quickly and hold no resentment. It's a wonderful gift when you can trust your friends and know that they love you for being you. It is these qualities that make it comfortable and enjoyable to be with them. For these reasons I treasure my friendships."

 ## Five Ways to Judge Whether a Girlfriend Lets Us Be Genuine

1. Do I pretend to be someone I'm not?
2. Do I worry about what to say to her?
3. Do I feel I have to live up to an image?
4. Do I feel pressured when I am around her?
5. Does she try to change me?

If the answer to any of these is yes, perhaps we should reexamine that friendship. A true friend is one who likes us for who we really are, faults and all.

Being ourselves means more than foregoing lipstick and choosing comfy but not-so-stylish pants. It also means trusting our friends with the very things that make us human: imperfection. Gabriela knows that if she says or does something stupid around her friends, it will still be OK. "Sometimes I am worried that I will say or do a stupid thing and everyone will laugh at me, but if I do, I always end up laughing about it myself, and it turns funny instead of stupid. A year ago, when my family got a new car, I was trying to impress all my friends with the things it could do. I realized that it wasn't such a big thing, and I should be talking about mutual interests instead of boasting about something less important. I have friends of all different economic backgrounds and, after thinking about it for a while, I realized that not only was it uninteresting conversation, but it might also hurt someone's feelings. I feel that I like being with my friends and they like being with me, and I don't have to impress them to get their attention."

She Is Like a Sister

"A best friend is a sister destiny forgot to give us," writes Lin. "She's the sister I never had" is a common refrain among teen girlfriends. Girlfriends can be like sisters — without our parents having to remind us to like each other. These "sisters" share a bond of closeness, not blood. When we need them, they are there. Friends who are like sisters are described as girls who are similar to us, who share our clothes and other things, who enjoy spending time with our families, and who truly are committed to staying close to us. Although they also "fight like sisters," getting into minor or serious fights, they always are able to make up and move on afterward. Interestingly, some girls say their friend who is like a sister is *not* necessarily their best friend.

Rhiannon does consider her best friend to be a soul sister. "No matter what happens, we can tell each other everything and give each other advice. We are always there for each other. A best friend is someone who you can tell all your hopes, dreams, goals, worries, crushes, and breakups. She also is there for you when you need a shoulder to cry on and understands and forgives your moods and quirks. She's the sister I never had (but always wanted!). We've both been in the position to tell each other we would be so much better without certain guys and to move on with our lives. And we have both gone to each other crying when we realized that it's actually over and we had to face things alone for a while. When that happened to me it was really hard, and she helped me through it by reminding me of all the reasons I ended it every time I talked about missing being with him."

Nikole describes how her friend is so much like a sister that she even blends in with her own family. "Brittany seems like a sister to me because I can tell her anything. It just so happens that I have a sister, Traci, and all three of us are best friends. We do everything together! I never ask if she can come to outings with our family anymore because my mom loves her also. If she misses an event, everyone wants to know where she is!"

Jessica says her friend Lisa and she are so much like sisters that they "share" each others' mothers. "We share clothes, the same friends, and similar hatred for our jobs. We color our hair together, and we even call each other's mom 'Mom.'" Trinity remembers feeling like she was part of her friend Lindsay's family. "When I was still living in Jersey, I was *always* at her house being part of the family. It was like they actually loved me in a way I didn't get at home."

From Jessica's Yearbook:

Love ya like a sister!

Except I fight with my sister over the hairdryer, and I don't with you.

Except my sister steals my clothes from my closet, but you ask first.

Except my sister would rather spend time with her boyfriend than with me, but you'd choose me—or at least not treat me as second best.

Except I didn't choose my sister, but I chose you as my friend.

FF! Love, Gianina

Jamie compares her feelings of responsibility to one of her friends as the feelings a big sister would have toward a younger one. "My friend Kristin is like a little sister to me. I feel totally responsible for her, even though she doesn't always take my advice. She's only a few months younger than I am, but she is a lot less concerned with her future, so we're kind of perfect for each other. She's always helping me to loosen up more, and I'm helping her to think more about her actions and their consequences. We tell each other every little thing about certain subjects, be it about making out with a guy or feeling worried about relationships with family members."

Of course, sisters don't always get along so perfectly all of the time. Yet with sisters, we know that no matter how much we bug them, how much we fight, they will always be around. And so it is with some of our friends. "My friend Jenna and I are definitely the sister type," says Laura. "We have that relationship where we share our clothes and makeup and hair stuff and whatever else. We are always together and our families are very close too. Sure we fight, but when we do, it is in a sisterly way. We forgive and forget the next day. And that's why sometimes I feel like it's OK to fight with her because I know everything will be OK afterward. I feel like she is my sister and that I can treat her like a sister. I know sometimes I hurt her and she knows she sometimes hurts me, but we know that, no matter what, we will always be friends."

Kristin and her best friend actually might even become sisters—at least, sisters-in-law. "I met Amanda through my sister's boyfriend. We are as close as sisters now. In fact, we might become sisters because my sister and her brother plan on getting married! Yeah!"

Share and Share Alike

One of the ways we show our trust is by sharing our most sacred possessions with our friends. "We share our thoughts, our ideas, and our secrets with our friends. But don't forget—girlfriends share their stuff!" Jennifer e-mails. "My stuff is her stuff" is a common refrain among friends. "I love to share clothes with my friends," Angel laughs. "It's one of the great things about being a girl. You can share clothes and CDs and whatever else you want. Sometimes you might have to persuade them to let you borrow their stuff, but it always works out. The secret is to let them borrow whatever and whenever they want from you!"

Laura agrees, and has seen her wardrobe double as a result. "My friend Jenna and I share clothes all the time. Half the stuff in my closet is her clothes. We would borrow them but never give them back, and we are OK with it. I love sharing clothes with her because it's a new style for both of us." Zoe has had a similar experience: "I have almost a whole closet of my best friend's clothes. She lent them to me way back when, and I still have them. I have a habit of taking my friends' clothes, but they don't seem to care. They all have my clothes, too, so it evens out. I mean you can't *not* share at boarding school. You basically don't have anything personal. Everyone shares *everything!*"

 Top Five Things Moon Shares with Her Girlfriends

1. Clothes
2. CDs
3. Money (when one of us is broke)
4. Shoes (helps to be the same size)
5. Homework (perhaps I shouldn't admit that one)

Is nothing sacred with our best friends? Not everyone shares everything with everybody. Nikole believes some things should be off limits to other people, with the exception of—who else—her girlfriends. "I share, but only with my very best friends who I trust with anything. Videos, video games, CDs, clothes, bracelets, hair clips, food, drinks, and even a brother or sister to get something done (joke, joke!)." Some friends get extra-special privileges, as Joy tells us. "Elaine and I are both pretty wary of our CDs. I don't let anyone else touch my CDs, but for some reason we have no problem sharing our CDs with each other. And that kind of runs into other things, too. Elaine drives this classic car, a '72 Super Beetle, and it is her pride and joy. She offered to teach me how to drive it because it is a semiautomatic, and no one drives her car. No one."

Sharing our most treasured possession is a sign of ultimate trust. "One of my friends gave me her favorite necklace as a good luck charm," tells Trinity. "And I gave her my favorite bracelet so she had a good luck charm, too. So far her necklace helped me find a boy I'm sorta dating and my bracelet helped her pass a really hard midterm she had to take. After a night of me trying to help her study, she was getting absolutely nowhere. So I gave it to her the morning before the test. Later she found out she did much better than she usually does."

Sometimes we want to share with our friends, but we don't expect anything from them in return. Sarek told this story about how she and her friends share with a friend who isn't as fortunate as they are. "One of my friends lives with a foster family who is poor and doesn't treat her very well. My other friends noticed that she wasn't eating lunch and figured out she didn't have enough money to buy it. So we decided to alternate paying for her lunch or bringing extra of our own. But we don't want her to feel ashamed, so we try to do it so she really doesn't notice. Like, I will buy an extra sandwich and then say, 'I'm not going to eat this, do you want it?' Or we all swap what we brought and pretend not to notice she has nothing to share."

Our belongings may be just material things, but when we share them with others they represent more. They represent that we trust our friends to take care of them as we would. We trust our friends to give them back to us, even if it is only someday. And, because we let our friends hold on to our belongings, we show we trust that we will also be holding on to these friends.

Admiration

A friendship can have its beginning when we recognize a quality in a girl that we admire. We see something in her that we want to be close to and that we want to have for ourselves. Alisa told us about the different qualities she admired in each of her closest girlfriends. "I admire honesty in Tiffany. I know that I can always count on her to tell me the truth. I like that Meghan knows how to have a good time and be silly. She also knows how to stand up for people that she cares about. Crystal doesn't care what people think. I think that that is important because she is herself all of the time."

When we admire a quality in a friend, we can learn from her and emulate it. Cecily remembers herself as a girl, too buttoned up and fragile until her friend helped her break through her fears. "My friend Brianna has shown me how to be strong but still be true to being a girl," says Cecily. "She has shown me you can be a lady without being a wimp. She is into many sports, including track, karate, and basketball. Yet she is polite and diplomatic and carries herself with poise, not to mention she is very smart and strong. I try to be more like her—a lady, but a modern lady."

 ## Five Things That Nikole Admires about Brittany

1. The way she speaks her mind
2. The way she is kind and gentle to her friends and even to people she doesn't like
3. The way she carries and presents herself
4. The way she pursues her dream, even when it seems impossible
5. The way she puts her friends above almost everything else and will lend a hand in any time of need

Marianna admires the strength of character of her friend Gitty. "One of my very good friends, named Gitty, suffers from a terrible physical disability. Gitty is blind and cannot walk normally. She was born with a hole in her spinal cord. Then she lost her sight in a car accident when she was in sixth grade. It is beyond painful to see such a lovely young woman with such a disability. We've known each other since junior high. I talk to her a lot and try to help her out as much as I can. It always pains me to know that no matter how much I try to help her, I will never be able to give her her sight back or cure her.

"Gitty is very strong, and she deals with her disability very boldly. She takes care of herself and tries to teach others to do the same. She's one of the bravest people I know. I envy her courage and power of will to keep going and to overcome all the barriers her disability establishes in her way. I just wish that I could do something to give her her sight back, so she could see all the beautiful things in the world. I wish I could make her walk normally and not have metal stuck in her knees. It's just really difficult to know that she's faced with such a challenge every day and that there's nothing she can do about it. I really am thankful to Gitty for showing me strength, courage, and power of will to deal with challenges. I just hope someday I can repay her for all the kindness and grace which she has shown me."

These stories showcase one of the best things we gain from friendships. We learn from other people's best qualities, adopting them for ourselves or simply just enjoying them. Alisa appreciates the best qualities in her friends that they share with others. Cecily emulates her friend's style. And Marianna recognizes that, by being around Gitty, she can absorb her friend's strength and goodness and become a better person just by being near her.

There is a fine line between admiration and envy, however. We know the friend, the one who is taller or has better hair than we do, who is funnier or gets better grades, who can talk to guys without freezing up or is captain of the sports team. *That* friend.

"*That* friend is Mackenzie," says Priya. "Everyone likes her. She gets good grades. She is a good athlete. She is so gorgeous she is in TV commercials. You want to hate her, but she is so nice you can't."

Katie Lou admits that, at times, she is jealous of her longtime friend Ames for two reasons. "Ames has a lot more money and more friends than I do. I have my close-knit group of friends and not a *whole* lot of money. But we were friends way before we knew how much our daddies made, so the money issue doesn't play a huge role in the friendship. As far as friends go, I know that my friends are true, while her friends are more of the 'fakey' friends. But when she has someplace to go on Friday night, and I'm sitting at home, that makes me more than slightly envious." Alisa knows that feeling. "I'm really close friends with this girl Crystal. Now let me just say that she is something else, just beautiful. Wherever I go with her, there is bound to be somebody stopping and asking her for her phone number or something. I know I sound jealous, but the truth is, sometimes I feel lucky to be walking down the street with her."

It is only natural to feel jealous of others, including our friends. How we deal with it shows our true character. We can learn to turn envy into a more positive quality for our friendship: admiration. We can admire our friend's athletic skills, and it can inspire us to practice harder at our favorite sport. We might not be able to have our friend's gorgeous hair, but we can admire it without feelings of bitterness. We can compliment our friend on her assets and truly mean it. Kristin has learned to go beyond her jealousy and take pride in her friend's achievements. "I have been jealous of my friend when we were younger, but I think you need to grow out of that. Jealousy is the worst feeling in the world. I believe jealousy caused our problems before in our friendship, which led to our not talking for more than two years. I have learned that you are what you are and to be happy with that. She has her unique characteristics and I have mine. I have learned to be happy for what she gets, and vice versa."

Marianna has a friend with whom she is in constant competition. She has learned to turn what could have been a negative into a positive. "I get very competitive with one of my close friends named Ella. We've always competed with each other with our clothes, school, guys, and especially grades. We would compare marks after each test to see who scored higher. But I always envied Ella because when she wants something, she will let nothing stand in her way. We both have high goals. She plans to become a lawyer or a businesswoman, and I plan to be a writer. I used to fear I wouldn't get what I want, but now I have been more active in building the basis for my career. I have become more confident of my success. In a way, I owe it to Ella because she has inspired me to do better than I thought I could and has showed me the importance of fighting for what I want."

When we recognize a quality of our friend that we envy, we can learn from our feelings. We discover what we really want. For our girlfriends, we turn jealousy into genuine pride in our friend. We can turn competitiveness into truly being happy for the friend who beats us. And when we do, we bind our friendships even closer.

Our Biggest Fan

It seems that just at that moment when we begin to think, "I can't do this," our girlfriends come along to offer their strength and comfort. A friend can be our most supportive cheerleader, our toughest coach, and our good luck charm all in one. Her advice and support help carry us through when we think we might fail. She'll kick us off the bench when we spend too long warming it. When a girlfriend is there to cheer us on, we feel empowered and can do better than we ever imagined. Our girlfriends who support us can make all the difference in the world.

❊   ❊   ❊

"My friend Megan comes to my track meets, and I go to her lacrosse games to cheer each other on," says Katelyn. "I'll be running and then I'll hear 'Go Katelyn!' from the stands. She gets all the people, even if they don't know me, to cheer me on."

Michalea's friends appreciate her attitude. "Even though I don't play many sports, I think it is important to go to my friends' games and show support for them. I've gone to watch their basketball games, even though I hardly know anything about the sport."

"My friends and I go to the B basketball games and cheer our friends on," says Paige. "Everyone goes to see the A team play, but no one goes to the B team so we want to support them. We hold up signs for Jennifer, Jenée, and Rachel and yell and cheer for them so much I lose my voice. We are our own peanut gallery."

Betsy's friend knows how to make everyone on the team feel supported. "After every game, Tally will go around to each person and say 'Good job!' 'Good job!' It doesn't matter if you didn't play well or even if you didn't play at all. Tally will make everyone feel like they are part of the team."

Marianna's girlfriend's support gave her the encouragement to follow one of her dreams. "Tanya is an artist, currently studying in art school. I have always looked up to Tanya because this was a girl who showed me strength and courage. She goes after what she wants. I love writing short stories, articles, and books. My dream is to become a well-known writer someday. I wanted to get my work published but was too scared to try to accomplish this goal. I guess I wasn't too secure in my ability to write well. Recently, after having a long conversation with Tanya, I began to feel inspired by her attitude and confidence. I decided to try to pursue my goals and publish my work. Sure enough, after a lot of editing of my work made by my English teacher, I sent my work to a web site. And before I knew it, my wish had come true; I was finally published. I am now a recognized author on a major web site. I am grateful to Tanya for bringing out the qualities of courage, strength, hard work, and power of will to be able to accomplish my goal. I thank her for giving me the inspiration to go after what I want."

It is a characteristic of girls to downplay their successes. "Oh, it was nothing," we might say. "Anyone could do it." Girlfriends don't let us get away with any of that thinking. When Lin succeeded, her friends forced her to be proud of her accomplishment. "I took the SATs on a whim this fall, even before my PSATs. I opened the envelope with the results, not expecting much since I hadn't studied or prepared. I couldn't believe my score, a 1480. I didn't tell anyone at first, then I shared my score with Christina. I started to play it down, you know, "It's no big deal. It's just a fluke." But she wouldn't let me. She dragged all of our friends over to me, and they were screaming and jumping up and down and picking Ivy League colleges for me. That night they took me out to eat at a nice restaurant to celebrate. The only bad part is, when I complain about being stupid, one of them whips out my SAT score and with that they try to make me feel smart again. It even works sometimes."

There are times when we think we are going to lose our nerve, we are going to choke, we are going to screw it up. Then a friend comes along and gives us the boost we need at just the right moment. Katie and her friend Lindz know they can count on each other to gear them up for the game. "Lindz and I have been on the same volleyball team, and we can usually tell when the other one is nervous. Just before the game, we tell each other we are 'da glue, meaning the glue that sticks together so neither of us will fall apart. It gets our confidence going. And then we have an awesome practice and an awesome game."

Melissa's girlfriend encouraged her to go to the cheerleading tryouts even if it meant taking a potential spot away from her. "Markie urged me to try out for the cheerleading squad at school because she said that I was good enough to make it. I didn't believe her in the slightest! She said that she just wanted me to humor her and do it, so I did it. When we found out who made the squad, I was on the list. But I didn't want to be a cheerleader, so I turned the position down so someone who really wanted it could do it. But it was nice to know I could."

The best girlfriends are there to cheer you on not only when you win, but when you lose. Laura's friend Erin helped her through the ups and downs of cheerleading tryouts. "I was going crazy all day long at the cheerleading tryouts. Cheerleading was my life. It was the only thing I thought I was really good at and had done for so long. I had been in cheerleading for seven years, and I would have been real upset if I didn't make the high school squad. My friend Erin, who was also trying out, helped calm me down. She told me to just go out there and try my best. She said, 'Don't think about the judges sitting there in front of you. Just pretend like you are by yourself, and you'll do just fine.' So I did just that. I thought I did OK, but I didn't make the squad. But my best bud Erin was right there for me all the way. She told me to just keep trying and work hard and next year I was sure to make it. She told me no matter what, I would always be the number one cheerleader to her."

Jessica's friend helped her recognize that she should do her best even when she didn't get what she wanted. "About a year ago, I was in the play *Snow White and the Seven Dwarfs*. I was kind of upset because I had auditioned for the parts of Snow White and the evil queen, but I got the part of the old hag who gives Snow White the poisonous apple. It was a really small part. My only scene was about three minutes long. I was pretty bummed about that. At rehearsals, I would sit and wait for hours just to practice my one and only scene. My friend Lisa, who was coming to see me in the show, surprised me with a present. It was a little figure of my character, the old hag, holding a basket of apples. It was the coolest gift ever because it helped me remember that my character was really important, even if it was the smallest part in the whole play. Lisa didn't know how much her little gift meant to me. I keep it on my dresser all the time, and it has helped me with other small roles I have played since then."

 Five Ways Jessica R's Girlfriends Support Her

1. They come to all of my plays.
2. They help me write my Oscar acceptance speech.
3. They talk about me as if I'm already famous.
4. They call me after auditions to find out how it went.
5. They include me in their lists of favorite actresses.

When our knees are trembling and butterflies attack our stomach—but we have to face the audience—a good friend can nudge us toward the stage, giving us a sense of confidence. Alisa told us how her friend Rhonda helped her get over her fear of performing with a solid piece of advice. "We sing at my church. Well, the first time we were about to sing, I got so nervous, I was shaking and stuff. She told me not to worry about it because she would be right next to me the whole time. She was like, 'Hey, this is worship. You can even close your eyes and get away with it.' So I did. And I felt much better."

Nikole's friend Summer gave her a much-needed pep talk. "I had a speech for a PTA meeting coming up that I was very nervous about. It ran about two minutes and I hate to speak in front of people. My good friend Summer, a natural actress/speaker, gave me some tips that helped me through the speech. She told me to look just above everyone's heads and to think that it would be over in a few minutes. Lastly she said that we're all human and that we make mistakes, and even if I did flub up no one would care because they'd be listening to my message and not the way I delivered it. It was great advice, and I thank her for it even now." Sarah's friend Susan recognized that the best way to shine in the spotlight is to be prepared. "Susan would say the line before mine and if I said the right line and if I got all of them right, she would take me out to lunch. Then we acted out the whole play, and she did everybody's parts except for mine."

A girlfriend who supports us when we need her is our solid ground when we are shaky on our feet. With the motivation of her friend, Marianna became a published writer and made a dream come true. Morgan and Katie play ball, knowing they have a fan in the stands cheering them to victory. And Laura's friend cheered her on and cheered her up when victory turned to defeat. With our girlfriends' encouragement, we make self-discoveries that enable us to grow and realize our fullest potential.

Reality Check

One of the lessons to be learned from friendship is who and what makes a true friend. Our judgment isn't always 100 percent accurate, but time tells which friendships are the ones worth holding on to. When our friends have hard times, we support them. When a friend participates in harmful and illegal behaviors, we can let her know what she is doing is wrong. We can try to help her and try to help her get help. But it's a different story when a friend doesn't listen. And when she tries to steer us in the wrong direction, it becomes a whole different story. We deserve to be treated with respect and must hold our friends accountable for their actions. When a friend continues to encourage us to do things we know we shouldn't, the strongest among us knows that it is time to let her go.

"Everyone has friends who aren't the best influences on you at one time or another," Aisha says. "But it is up to you to stay strong and not participate in the wrong behavior. And then to decide whether it is worth hanging around these people when there are so many people with better friend potential out there."

Nikole remained strong around her friends who were wrong for her and has wise advice. "I have had friends that were bad for me. After discovering what was 'bad' about them, I had a choice to make: continue our friendship or find better friends. The latter was the choice I made. Friends shouldn't expect you to do something to make them happy. Any friendship should make someone happy."

 ## Five Signs of a Soon-to-Be Ex-Friend

1. She puts you down and makes you feel bad about yourself.

2. She talks you into dangerous and wrong situations.

3. She seems happy when you fail and jealous when you succeed.

4. She wants you to act and dress like her and do only what she wants to do.

5. She consistently "takes" more than she "gives."

Jamie has changed her friends when she saw them going astray. "I used to hang out with people who would've been bad for me. If I'd respected them I would have lost respect for me. As it is, I think they're all going to end up working at convenience stores, so I haven't gone along with them when skipping school, drinking, or driving with an underaged driver has come up. My friend Tiffany would do some of that, but I've made her realize how stupid all that junk is, and she's no longer interested."

When a so-called friend pressures us into doing things that we would never dream of doing, we realize that she is not a friend at all. Marianna tells a frightening story of how her friend led her into potential danger. Her friend Emily talked her into leaving a party with two guys Marianna didn't know. Marianna went along because she trusted Emily's judgment. Emily told Marianna they just had to pick someone up, and they would be back in fifteen minutes. Hours later, Marianna was still being driven around, with her questions about going back to the party ignored. Finally, the guys stopped at a motel, and Marianna continued to go along with her supposed friend. "I sat down on the bed next to Emily, who at that time (as I had just begun to figure out) had taken an ecstasy pill. She hardly knew what she was doing. I told her I wanted to leave the motel and get back to the party. She said no, she wanted to stay.

"It was only then that I began to realize that the sweet, innocent Emily had set me up big time! Emily couldn't care less about hanging out with me that night. She was using me as bait for her own motives to be with one of the guys. Since there were two guys, they wanted another girl to accompany them to the motel room. I found out they had reserved it in advance. Emily had known that we would not be back in fifteen minutes, but she lied anyway. She just needed an excuse to get me to go with them. She knew that after I got into their van, it would already be too late to change my mind. I realized now how naive I had been all this time, thinking that Emily and I could be good friends, trusting her every word, and believing that I was not in any danger. In reality, her word meant nothing. Emily defied my trust and betrayed our friendship. She used me and couldn't care less what would happen to me once her goals of being with this guy and his drugs were fulfilled.

"A friend is supposed to be there for you through hard times, not bring you purposely to face them. A friend is supposed to care what happens to you and not put you in any danger. Then again, as I have seen many times before, not every friend is a true friend. Considering the circumstances, I didn't know whether I'd be raped or even murdered. I didn't trust any of them, especially Emily. I feared that I had gotten myself into such trouble that I might never get out of it. Life is such a mystery sometimes, you just never know who to trust. Your own friend could risk harming you without you even knowing it." How could a friend do such a thing? Marianna asks. Of course, the answer is that Emily was not a true friend. And we have to let go of the illusions of some friendships and face reality straight on. We can gather our courage and find someone else who is truly worthy of being called our friend.

Positive Influences

The people we choose to surround ourselves with influence our lives. We've all heard the term peer pressure, where your peers try to influence you to do something. But peer pressure isn't always bad. There is such a thing as positive peer pressure, when a friend encourages you to do the *right* thing. Our parents call these friends Good Influences. We recognize that these friends are looking out for us, so we are and will become the best that we can be.

Elizabeth describes how her friends encourage her to challenge herself. "My friends are able to console me when I bomb a test or when I make a fool out of myself. But then they encourage me to study for the next test or get over the embarrassment. They'll listen to my problems and give me the honest advice I need. They also encourage me to try new things that I normally wouldn't try, like rock climbing, or going out on a Friday night when I'm feeling lazy."

Jamie's friend's encouragement has led her to pursue a whole new direction in life. "My friend Claire is trying out for a nearby arts high school. One time she offhandedly told me I should try out too, since we both love our choir class so much. Since she told me about it, I've been falling in love with that school. We just toured it, and now I'm officially hooked. She's helped me to realize how much passion I have rotting away in myself that could be put to better use."

Our friends can help us build on our weaknesses and overcome them. Jess tells us, "I have one friend who encourages me to stand up for myself. I have become a stronger person in the last year. Because of her I don't doubt myself as much as I used to." Harmony admits she puts herself down too often and her friend Kim was tired of it. "I was always talking about how stupid I am, so my friend Kim made a T-shirt that she would wear whenever I called myself stupid too often. It was one of those 'I'm with Stupid' shirts. So I would know when I was too down on myself."

Melissa's friend hung tough to help her kick the smoking habit. "My friend Markie sets me straight all the time. I started smoking, and she brought to my attention how bad it really was. She would make sure there was no way for me to get any cigarettes. She talked to me and filled my time so I had no time to smoke. She helped devise ways so I wouldn't need one. Every time I needed a cigarette, she would tell me to hit her as hard as I could, because me smoking was causing her pain anyway. Eventually I got sick of hurting her and the other people around me, and I just quit."

Trinity looks back with deep regret at a time when her friend tried to be a positive influence and she disregarded it. "Jaysey gave me the great ultimatum: drugs or her and her posse. She knew what direction I was heading in, and she gave me the choice. I chose to get in the car with the people who decided pot was more important. She had given me a choice, drugs or her. I've been through a year of rehab. It's pretty obvious I made the wrong decision."

Caring enough to tell it to you straight is the sign of a real girlfriend. When it would be easier to tell you what you want to hear, they care enough about you to tell the truth. They help you see it for yourself and then guide you back in the right direction. When Melissa, Stephanie, and Trinity were at their lowest, their friends were honest and didn't let up on them until they did the right thing.

Celebrating
Our
Friendships

When we think about some of the times we have spent with our girlfriends, we smile, we laugh, and sometimes we even cringe in embarrassment. Part of the joy of friendship is feeling comfortable being silly, celebrating good times, and sharing our pleasures. We throw parties; we share gifts for special occasions or "just because"; we enjoy eating and cooking with one another. We find ourselves singing at the tops of our lungs together and heading out on the open road for the all-girlfriend adventure. These are the times we will remember for the rest of our lives.

Being Crazy

What is the number one thing we like to do with our friends? Have fun, of course! Being a teen brings with it constant pressures from which we all need a release. Sometimes we just need to kick back, let our hair down, and be outright silly. One way some girls let themselves go is to shed their trendy clothes and dress themselves up.

"My friends and I dress up in really weird clothes," says Alicia. "We'll wear old costumes from Halloween, from old dance recitals, and anything obnoxious. Then we go to Limited Too and put on all this body glitter and gels from the testers. We walk around the mall, and people think we are crazy."

Katelyn and her friend dressed up and went out in public—but not on purpose. "My friend and I were dog sitting, and she accidentally let him out of the house. We chased him a couple of blocks. All these people driving by were beeping at us and calling out to us, and we just thought it was about the dog. Then we got home and my mother started laughing. We forgot we had been playing around earlier putting on all this makeup and crazy stuff. So we were running around my neighborhood looking like that!"

Laura and Shayna dress up, too. But it's a good thing they stayed home when they dressed like this: "Shayna was spending the night at my house, and we were really bored. It was 3:30 in the morning but we weren't tired. So we decided to dress weird and take pictures of ourselves. Well it just so happened she had an Eeyore bra and I had an Eeyore stuffed animal. I had a Tigger bra and, you guessed it, a Tigger stuffed animal. So we put the bras on our heads and held up the stuffed animals and took pictures. Hey, you get crazy thoughts in your head at 3:30 in the morning."

Zoe and her friends have a huddle. "When we need to decide something because the rest of our group or just ourselves sometimes can't decide, we huddle together with our heads touching. Then we whisper stuff, and we say break! We come up and Alex announces what we decided. It's kinda goofy; that's why we like it."

Janessa and her friends dressed up and gave themselves makeovers. "We pretended we were models on a shoot, and we had to do different themes like a summer shoot, a dance shoot, and a dressy shoot. Like for the dance shoot, we wore old dance costumes, like green velvet jazz pants and a green velvet belly shirt. Then we sent them to a modeling agency and got accepted. But it was too expensive and probably a scam anyway."

Shopping is a major activity among teen girlfriends, but they do more than just shop in the stores. Corin and her friend Janet do crazy things at Wal-Mart. "There is an Internet list going around that is 'Fifty Fun Things to Do at Wal-Mart.' You do crazy things like ride a bike around the store, walk through the clothing department and say really loudly, 'Who buys this crap anyway?' or drop on the floor and start screaming, 'The voices! The voices!' whenever the loudspeaker comes on, stuff like that. So we just go around Wal-Mart and try to do as much of that as we can. It's really fun because you're not hurting anyone, but people get a little freaked out."

Regarding what kinds of crazy things she does with her friends, Joanne says, "Two words, *picture booths!* We cram as many people as possible into those picture booths and get strips of us doing stupid, crazy things. One time, at night, we spent so long in the picture booth producing strips after strips that the mall closed on us. We had to get a janitor to let us out!"

And Patricia's response to that question? "Invisible Bill! One time my friend and I were eating at a pizza place, and we made up an imaginary friend who was really tiny. Invisible Bill. These guys sat in a seat behind us and we yelled at them, 'Watch out! You just squished Bill!' They got up and my friend took a cup and put 'Bill' in the cup. We pretended to give him CPR and stuff. When the guys were leaving, they went up to the counter and took the microphone and announced, 'Invisible Bill lives.' And they left us there in hysterics."

Part of what we love about our girlfriends is the way we can let loose with them and rediscover the child within us.

With some of our friends we can act like little kids again and do things we used to like to do in our childhood. Joanne and her friend Kim play house and hide-and-seek. "It's embarrassing, but we only recently stopped playing those games." Zoe went with her friend Risa to Chuck E Cheese and had pizza and played skeeball with all the little kids until it closed. Remember jumping on your bed when you were a kid? "Cassandra and I still do that every time she sleeps over. I have two twin beds, and we jump from one to another. I guess we refuse to give up being kids!" admits Annie.

Where do we come up with these ideas? However weird they are, we crack ourselves up when we do them. Melissa and her friend Markie go around and bark at people. "We make strange faces at them. It is really funny to see the reactions on the peoples' faces. I just hope we don't scar anyone for life!" Zoe is embarrassed to admit this, but "One time, a whole bunch of us sat around my friend Kath's house and made fart noises for a whole hour. And we couldn't stop laughing the whole time."

There have been occasions when our crazy ideas sounded good at the time, but proved to be not such good ideas after all. Grace learned this the hard way. "My friend Sarah and I were totally bored. The power had gone out because of a mild tornado that had blown by. Since there was no light at all, we decided to do something crazy. My friend Jacob was there, and, well, we both like him. So we were acting goofier than usual. Sarah came up with the idea. Since the power was out and it was dark, she dared me to run around outside butt naked. We both undressed and left our clothing on the front porch. We went out running. When we came back we found out that Jacob had locked us out and taken our clothes. We had to crawl through the bathroom window and walk around in towels until we found Jacob with our clothes. And, of course, the power was back on."

Jessica R. and her friends also experienced a good idea gone wrong. "Last summer, my friend Liz invited me and two of our friends to go swimming in her private lake that was on her family's property. We were swimming around for a while, just goofing around, when Jenn suggested we take the canoe out to the middle of the lake and jump off. So we hopped in the canoe, and Liz started paddling us out. But she couldn't control the boat, and we just kept going in circles, over and over. So I took over the oars. I couldn't steer us either, so we just kept passing the oars around. None of us could paddle right, and we weren't getting anywhere! Finally we made it out to the middle of the lake and decided we weren't going to go in the water because it was getting late.

"We were trying to row back in towards the beach, but all of a sudden we noticed that the canoe was filled with spiders. We all started screaming and jumping up, and the canoe capsized. We must've spent over an hour out in the middle of the lake, trying to tip the canoe upright again and bail all the water out. We kept saying 'We can't let the Titanic sink!' After a long time, we realized it is impossible to bail water out of a capsized canoe, so in the end the four of us had to swim all the way in, pulling and pushing the boat. It was the funniest thing ever, like something out of a movie. We couldn't stop laughing the whole time."

When we let loose together, we share experiences that really solidify our friendships. We indulge ourselves in the moment, letting go of our rational selves, and letting our alter egos reign. We are free to do as we please. These are the times when we create the unforgettable memories that we will treasure for the rest of our lives.

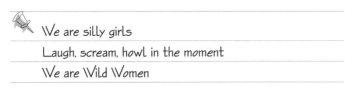

We are silly girls
Laugh, scream, howl in the moment
We are Wild Women

Celebrations

Who makes our celebrations memorable and meaningful? Our girlfriends, of course! Whether we are celebrating our birthdays or just celebrating ourselves, our friends make special times even more so. Birthdays are the perfect opportunity to celebrate our friends. After all, aren't our friends some of the best gifts we give ourselves? Katie Lou and her friends make a big deal about each other's birthday and want the world to know it. "For AT and Mary's birthdays, we all got together early in the morning and went to their house around 6:30 A.M. to wake them up. Then we dressed them up in hideous clothes and crepe paper, made them wear a sign saying 'Hey, Hey, It's My Birthday!' and then took them to breakfast."

Paige's friends gave her a surprise birthday party. "I thought I was just going out to eat. I showed up at the restaurant and saw a group of my friends. I was really surprised. I had to wear a corny party hat and carry balloons in my teeth. A fake policeman showed up and pretended to arrest me. He handcuffed me and read me my rights. It was fun."

Samantha's friends shared a birthday to remember. "I have my birthday around the same time as my friends who are twins, Renee and Carol. Our moms were picking us up from tae kwon do when they told us they were kidnapping us for our birthdays. We drove a couple hours and then pulled up to this incredible spa resort place. The moms pulled out overnight bags with our bathing suits and things and said we were going to stay there overnight. It turned out Renee's and Carol's aunt works there and got all these discounts on the rooms and stuff for us. We all got manicures, seaweed facials, and massages. We lay out by the pool and hung out in the hot tub.

We ate this huge dinner and then ordered room service at midnight. We felt like princesses. It was the best."

We don't need it to be someone's birthday to throw a celebration. We should take time every once in a while to celebrate our friendships. Sydney and her friends plan theme nights. "We threw Hawaiian parties and hung out in my friend Keely's hot tub outside. We decked out in leis, bought tropical candy, rented beach movies, sipped nonalcoholic fuzzy navels, and 'swam' in the hot tub. We ended up camping out in Keely's FROG(Finished Room Over Garage). It was tons of fun." While Sydney goes tropical, Char and her friends go Mexican. "My best friends and I had a fiesta. We had Mexican food, drank alcohol-free margaritas, and swam in my pool."

Joy tells us about a unique celebration she has with her friends. "We have Last Night on Earth parties. If someone's going away or something huge has happened to them like an award or something, we have this party. It's called Last Night on Earth because you're supposed to do everything you would do if it was your last night on earth. Clever, huh? Usually we all get gifts and just dance and joke around and have fun, but to the extreme."

Trinity tells about plans for a Girl's Night at her house the upcoming weekend. "My parents are going out of town and leaving me the house, so this is a good alternative to throwing a huge party and getting busted. We're renting videos. We're probably gonna just pig out with some pizza from the local pizza joint that has the world's *best* pizza. We'll probably dye our hair and just talk about life, love, relationships, sex, drugs, and music . . . and just have fun doing silly stupid things."

 ## Five Reasons Jamie and Her Girlfriends Celebrate

1. Snow day! We can go get Chinese for lunch while prices are low!

2. We have our periods! We have an excuse to be annoying and eat chocolate!

3. I asked someone out I barely know! It doesn't matter if he said yes or no!

4. International Friendship Day! (August 1)

5. We ran the mile in gym! We're still alive!

Celebrating major holidays with our friends makes them that much more fun. "Last year, Kate and I went caroling, and collected our other friends along the way," Allison says. "Eventually we had eight people in my little extended cab truck. It was great! We literally dragged a few friends out of bed, and we all had Santa hats. Well, except for me. I had bunny ears. That was Kate's fault though, she took my Santa hat. We knocked on random doors and sang, and banged on friends' windows . . . an absolute blast. "

Stephanie planned a Valentine's Day celebration with her friends Alyssa and Lindsay, who are sisters, which involved both of their families. "One of my favorite times I had with them was a few years ago on Valentine's Day. We wanted to do something nice for our parents. For a few weeks we planned what we were going to do. We chose a menu, prepared dinner and dessert, served them, and even cleaned the dishes! For entertainment, we decided to perform a short play that one of our mutual friends wrote. Everyone had a small part, including our younger siblings. Since several of us play instruments, in one of the scenes we played some background music. We had practiced for three weeks so we would be prepared. Everything worked out wonderfully! The parents were very appreciative, and it was fun too!"

When we celebrate with our friends, we are celebrating not only a special occasion, but our friendships. Think of each happy birthday song sung, each toast of the nonalcoholic drinks, each secret and laugh shared late at night as a testament of love to our friends.

Sleepovers

The classic all-girl party? The slumber party. Sleeping over at a friend's house gives us a whole night of potentially uninterrupted fun and bonding. "To me, a slumber party isn't a real slumber party when people go to sleep. The best slumber party is staying up all night, getting told continuous times to 'Go to sleep!' by adults," laughs Joanne.

"Silly" seems to be a buzzword when describing slumber parties. Jessica tells how she and her friends act silly at their sleepovers. She and her friends sleep out on her trampoline. "We take the thickest, warmest blanket each of us owns. We just talk for hours and hours. One time we were all asleep, and at 4:00 A.M. my sprinklers came on and soaked us. Usually we get scared when we hear noises and run inside. But if we're lucky, and are able to sleep, the last one up gets bounced up!"

Allison and her friends Kate, Sarah, and Taylor capture their slumber party memories on film. "We make these huge, elaborate movies then watch them at the next party just to see how dumb we were. And we make films of us sitting around and confessing things. We film all our talks so we never lose what we learned about each other or the feelings we had at that particular slumber party. It's funny to see the things that we talked about and what kind of information was divulged at three in the morning!" Aneri also videotaped a slumber party she had with her friends, but it was less meaningful and more just plain silly. "In ninth grade, I threw a 'We Hate 'NSync' slumber party with my close friends. I dressed up as Lance, my best friend as JC, and the others were Chris, Joey, and Justin. Then we videotaped us with this version of the movie *Scream* where all the members of 'NSync die, along with

Britney Spears, and Ricky Martin was kidnapped because he is the sexiest man alive. It was hilarious."

Teressa shared her funniest sleepover memory. "I was sleeping over at my friend Desiree's house with some of my friends. We all had crashed when all of a sudden Desiree wakes me up and points over to Jillian's sleeping bag. I heard this laughing and we went over. She was totally asleep but giggling really loud. I mean, *really* loud. I woke up my other friends, and we were all cracking up. Then all of a sudden, in this really flirty way, she goes, 'Darius!' And then Desiree screams, 'Darius? Darius, *my little brother?! Ewwww!*' That woke Jillian up and we told her what happened. She was totally embarrassed and Desiree just kept going, 'My *brother? Ewwww!*'"

The sleepover is one of the best places to really bond with a friend. Late at night, when the lights are low, we become not only tired, but talkative. We express our feelings more openly, and the stories flow. Char and her friends use slumber parties as a way to strengthen their friendships.

"We do something called Mail Time, where we all write letters to each other telling the other person how we think the friendship is going. If they have something good or bad to tell someone, Mail Time is when we do so. One time Brooke wrote me a letter during Mail Time about the time we went in my brother's convertible, driving around at night. Our hair was blowing back. We were laughing and screaming and listening to music. It was times like this I realize I couldn't ask for better best friends. One time I wrote my other friend a letter telling her about whenever I see her I smile, because she is so nice and sweet and funny. And I told her how in the mornings when I have to go to school, I just think of laughing with her so it will be OK and fun. She started to cry when she read it."

Slumber parties make us realize just how much we have in common with our girlfriends. We can be goofy, laugh until we cry, gossip, pig out, and give each other beauty treatments and new hair colors. More importantly, we talk and share our innermost secrets in moonlit heart-to-heart chats. There's something about those 3:00 A.M. gab sessions that forms an unbreakable bond between girlfriends. Whatever that something is, we're certainly glad it's there to remember always.

 Jessica R's Top Five Fun Things to Do at a Sleepover

| 1. Have a video marathon |
| 2. Camp out in the yard |
| 3. Make movies with the camcorder |
| 4. Go swimming at midnight |
| 5. Make prank phone calls |

Gifts from the Heart

One of the ways we show our friends we care is by giving them presents. But this doesn't mean we "buy" friendships. The presents that mean the most are not the most expensive. They are the gifts that come from our hearts. Alisa tells us, "I think gift giving is very important because it makes the person feel like they are important and special. Everybody likes to get gifts for themselves, but sometimes it's nice to just give to somebody for a change—especially if it is for no reason."

Joy's friend Elaine showed her how special she thought their friendship was by picking out a present that was just right for Joy. "Last year for Christmas Elaine got me a journal and a pen. It was great because I'd never gotten a journal before and I'm a writer. The pen is still my special pen, and no one else can use it. She also got me all of e.e. cummings's complete works and some other books. No one ever buys me books. It was so perfect."

Sometimes the best gift we receive is one that reflects how our friends are really paying attention to what is important to us. Homemade gifts show us that our girlfriends care enough about us to use their creativity to make us something one of a kind. Nikole says she likes to get and give homemade gifts. "It sounds really corny but they are the best. I like to receive homemade cards, mixed music tapes, a bouquet of flowers, a poem. I've given a candy basket, cookies, and cake to friends who went on vacation and some fudge to a friend who went to college." Laura agrees. "When I give my friends a gift for no reason at all it normally comes from the heart. I think a gift is better when it has more meaning to it. So just to thank my friends for what they have done, I often send them a poem or write them a note or something that comes from the heart and really lets them know how much they mean to me."

 Top Five Cheapo Things to Give to a Girlfriend

1.	Homemade cards
2.	Music CDs of mixes picked out for them
3.	Picture frames—with a photo of the two of you
4.	Food you baked yourself
5.	Friendship bracelet

Britt says she gives her friends gifts she has made all the time. "I think giving handmade things like friendship bracelets and stuff like that is the best way to show someone how much they mean to you." Paige and her friends also do friendship bracelets. "I choose their favorite colors and then think of which charms would suit them. For example, I might use a zodiac sign for their horoscope. I just made one for Lauren that is half dark blue, half yellow and has charms of a moon and stars."

Stephanie tells of her favorite gifts to give and receive. "For Christmas and Chanukah I make presents to give my friends. My grandfather makes jewelry and sends me lots of beads and string. Since I love to bead, some of my favorite gifts to give are beaded necklaces and bracelets. I also make pop-up cards, origami figures, and string bracelets. All of my friends have at least one thing I have made for them. It makes me feel good inside when I see something I made on someone else and know that she's enjoying it."

❄   ❄   ❄

Gabriela describes the gifts she and her friends have given each other. "They give me all kinds of gifts, from clothing to jewelry to self-made picture frames and origami boxes. The gifts that I cherish the most are those that are self-made. When I look back, those are the ones that I remember. When I received each of these wonderful, special gifts I felt a deep sense of friendship. For my thirteenth birthday, my mother had a Rites of Passage Celebration for me. We invited my close girlfriends and their mothers. My friend Stephanie made me a yarn figure of two girls embracing each other, depicting her and me. My friend Jessica made me a card that said such nice things about me, it made me want to cry. She used the letters of my name, *Gabriela*."

Generous to others
Amusing to be around
Beautiful, inside and out
Respectful
Intelligent
Everybody's friend
Lovable
Always there when you need her

Jess was touched by a simple gesture her friend Amanda made for her birthday. "Amanda made me the sweetest card for my seventeenth birthday. It had hearts and Bible verses about what love means. It said things like 'Love is patient,' and you lift the heart and it had a time when love was patient between she and I. There were ten of them on there. It was made of construction paper and everything. I will keep those till the day I die."

Jessica appreciated the sentiment in a card even more than she would have a present. "I tend to show my friends I care by giving them gifts. One Christmas, I pulled my friend Alice aside and explained to her that I had her Christmas present in the car, but I couldn't give it to her now. Looking a little embarrassed, she said to me that she didn't have a gift for me, but she had a homemade Christmas card! I was touched to hear this, since I always feel special when someone gives me a homemade card. Anyway, she gave me the card, and I opened it up and read it. Inside was the sweetest, most sincere message I have ever read. Since Alice is a bit reserved, and it took about a year before she really warmed up to me as a friend, this really meant a lot to me. It is one of the nicest Christmas gifts I have ever gotten: it was her friendship!"

Gifts don't need to cost a great deal of money. A book, a friendship bracelet, cookies, a homemade card—these are the gifts into which the giver puts a good deal of thought. What was most meaningful was when the gift was chosen because the giver just knew it was something a friend would cherish. And cherish them we do.

Making a Difference

Sharing our time with girlfriends is certainly important to developing and promoting our friendships. But when we spend time with our girlfriends while pulling together to help others, we add a whole new dimension to our friendships—and ourselves. Gabby and two of her friends started RAKA (Random Acts of Kindness Association). "Some of our acts have been handing out flowers to people who look sad and paying the toll for the car behind us."

Jenny and her friends banded together for a school community service project and discovered the true meaning of the holidays along the way. "There was a Christmas tree up at my school with names of children whose families couldn't afford presents that year. We could pick a name and buy a gift for the child. Four of my friends got together and pooled our money to buy a present for a six-year-old girl. We went to the toy store and decided on a bike. We wrote on the card, 'From Santa.' We all felt so good about doing that, and it was even more special because we shared that feeling together."

 ## Jenny's List of Simple Ways to Make a Difference

1. Collect donations for a cause
2. Clean up litter
3. Write a letter to the editor or to a politician
4. Pass around a petition
5. Volunteer your time

Isabel and her friends used their collective muscles to help families in need. "A boy in my school started a club that supported Habitat for Humanity. This is an organization where people help build houses for families who can't afford to buy homes. My friends Kayley and Michaela and I joined the club. We held a fundraiser to buy supplies. And then one Saturday we went out and helped a group of people build a house, hammering, lifting, sawing, and all."

When friends have a cause to support, there can be no stopping them. "There was an open lot near our school," tells Melissa. "It was just across the main road. A sign went up announcing there would be a Hooters built there. We didn't think the restaurant was appropriate so close to our school and other schools in the area. My friend Steffani and I wrote a letter to them telling them that they should build somewhere else. Her mom helped us make petitions that people could sign in protest." Jessica and her friend established a club to make a difference in the world. "My friend and I decided we wanted to start a Save the Earth club. We wanted to have weekly meetings and plan out what we could do to help the earth for that week. We would pick up litter and raise money for local animal shelters. I remember we would sit in our driveways after school and try to sell cookies and lemonade to the neighbors. We would sit there for hours and scream out to passing cars that we had 'cookies for a quarter!' The little money we made we always gave to charity. We called ourselves something like The Caring Club. We made all these signs that said stuff like, Stash the Trash! and Don't Drive Drunk! with our club's logo on it, and we would hang them up all over the neighborhood. The club was a really great idea, and I don't know when or why we stopped doing it. We both wanted to be little heroes and save the earth, or our town at least. I think we thought it was all up to us, because no one else in the neighborhood was taking any action. I think we got discouraged and gave up because there were only two of us in the club, and we couldn't get anyone else to join. But it was fun while it lasted!"

Aneri says she is an intense animal rights activist. "I have always been a vegetarian. My parents are also vegetarians so that was the way I was raised. Personally, I go a little beyond the belief system. I think not eating animals is the only way a person can truly *love* animals. If you truly love animals, then eating meat becomes almost cannibalism. A lot of my friends are animal lovers but eat meat. When I brought meatless lunches every day, my friends also started to question their eating habits. I explained about the cruelty in slaughterhouses (and what they are really eating) and mostly about how it's healthier. So one by one some of them stopped, too.

"Not *all* of my friends are vegetarians, and some of them love meat and can't give it up. I don't hate them for it; I just don't agree with them. The best part is that the friends that converted are also getting *their* friends to stop. I think it's great. Vegetarianism is healthier, beneficial, and reduces a significant amount of cancers. It's also proven that vegetarians live longer. Once in sixth grade, I was on a Girl Scout trip. It was my birthday, and the agenda was to fish and eat crabs. I put up a fight and did not want crabs to be killed on my birthday! Some supported, some did not. The leader finally said, 'OK, it's Aneri's birthday, we won't fish for crabs.' I was thrilled! About twenty girls couldn't kill crabs, and I consider it my biggest semi-vegetarian victory. I hope that more times will come again where I can make a difference, with people behind me."

Harmony and her friends use the Web as a forum to speak out for what they believe in. "My friend has this 'zine on the Web. Its purpose is to fight for human rights, especially the rights of teens because we don't really have any. It was started by a guy, but we girls have taken over and only let the guy put one or two things on it. Now it is a place for chicks. It is a place to voice our opinions and make some noise. It's not professional, but people read it and usually respond to what we've written."

Nikole and her friend Brittany have a plan to give back to their communities. "We would like to create a youth ministry and become youth ministers. I want to give something back to a country from which our generation has taken much. We've just thought of this idea at a recent youth rally at which two very talented guys were speakers. We think that we've all got at least one quality any kid can relate to. We are lucky that our lives have not included some of the dangers associated with teens today, but we wish to help those teens out. One of the biggest reasons to do this is it includes everything we want to do: travel, meet wonderful people, have fun together, and speak the word of the Lord. This would have to take place probably a few years after our high school graduation."

Spending time celebrating with our friends is wonderful and important to maintaining our friendships. But spending time with our friends helping others gives us something far deeper in common: a sense of moral good. It helps us tap our inner resources for someone else's benefit and, as an added bonus, it brings us closer to our girl-friends.

Shop 'til We Drop

When we head out for some girl time with our friends, one of the top destinations is definitely the mall. We go to buy, to try, and just to look. At the mall, we share more than just a mere shopping experience. When our friends help us try on clothes and jewelry, they help us see ourselves through someone else's eyes. When a friend says, "That is so *you*," we learn about more than just what fits well. Are we sporty or sophisticated, trendy or tried and true? Our friends help us try on our different identities and reveal more about ourselves.

"We're Mall Rats," laughs Tiana. "The mall is our second home." Marianna tells us that if she gets to choose what to do with her friends, the mall wins. "I love to go shopping with my friend Anna. Anna is definitely a future fashion designer, and she has the best taste in clothes. We help each other pick out clothes and listen to each others' opinions. I like to hear what she thinks looks good on me as well and get some new ideas."

Megan and her friend Allie love to shop, but they have to cater to each other's shopping style. "She is the kind of person who will buy something she likes at that very moment, while I have to think about it almost the entire time we are shopping and, most of the time, if I do decide to buy it I end up returning it."

 Alison's and Trinity's Fun Stuff to Do at the Mall with a Friend

1. Give people bad fashion advice in the dressing rooms

2. Pretend to argue with the voices in your head while she acts embarrassed

3. Play with the mannequins and put them into bizarre positions

4. Try on the UGLIEST outfits possible and hold a fashion show in the dressing room

5. Hide and go seek!

The mall isn't only a place to buy, it is a place to dream. "One of my favorite places to hang out with Brandi is at the mall," says Kim. "Even if we don't have any money, we go and window shop. We pick out things that we would wear if we were famous and going to the Grammy's or MTV Video Music Awards. Sometimes we pick out furniture and decorations we'd like to have in our future houses." And clothes and houses aren't the only thing they dream about at the mall. "We like to sit in the food court and scope out hot guys. When one of us sees a good-looking guy, we nudge the other one and smile. One guy had the most gorgeous face I had ever seen. Every time we go to the mall we look around for 'that guy' just in case. We swore to each other that next time we see him we'll at least talk to him."

Styles can clash at the mall, so friends have to be careful. Kim and her friend Brandi had to make a pact not to be offended by the other's opinion. "When we actually have money, we usually look for clothes. But Brandi is more colorful/retro, and I am more vintage/preppy. So when we go to look for clothes, we usually end up in complete opposite sides of the store. But then we ask for each other's honest opinions and thoughts on the clothes we pick out. But if you ask for an opinion, you can't be offended by the answer because you're the one who asked." Some girls avoid the mall with a particular friend because they end up driving each other crazy. Jamie likes to go to the mall to shop, but her friend Liz is into people spotting. "Liz and I used to always go to the mall, and as soon as she'd spaz about not seeing anyone she knew, she'd see a classmate and drag me all over the mall following them until they'd notice."

❄   ❄   ❄

The mall is more than just a place for us to buy things. It is an escape. We try on different personalities like Marianna, dream about the future or check out guys like Kim, and learn more about our friendships like Kim. The mall is like a mini-vacation for our minds that we get to share with our friends.

Nourishment

Food does more than nourish our bodies; it nourishes our soul. From sipping our mom's homemade soup when we are sick to sharing stories and laughter over a pizza lunch with red-and-white checked tablecloths, food brings strong emotional connections. It can satisfy us, comfort us, bring us together as we celebrate.

Going out to eat is near the top of our Things to Do List. We all have our fav places to eat. Priorities? They have to have: 1) people to see and be seen by and 2) cheap food. Food that tastes good ranked pretty low on the must-have list. "My friends and I go to Denny's, IHOP, Steak N Shake—any chain of diners with greasy food, basically!" says Katie Lou. "We pick those places because the food is cheap, and we have no money usually." Angel and Krista like to go to 7-Eleven to drink their slurpees. For Kim, it's french fries and Orange Juliuses at the food court. "My friends and I usually go for pizza, and we eat and eat until our stomachs are about to explode," laughs Betsy. For many others, fast food places topped the list.

Although it is definitely our favorite, eating isn't the only thing we like to do with our friends. Char and her friends have a cooking club. "One time when my four best friends were spending the night, we were up at two in the morning and we were hungry, but we wanted to eat something healthy and we wanted to cook. So Rachel said, 'Hey let's make salad,' and I said, 'No, we should make our very own salad dressing.' So we made it and put it in a cute bottle. It is so yummy we use it all the time. We make breakfast together in the mornings. We also cook noodles and pesto (our favorite) all the time."

Five Food Festivities

1. Learn to Cook Party—Enlist a girlfriend, or mom, who can teach you how to prepare a simple dish

2. Cake Decorating—Bake it and design it

3. Around-the-World Dinner—Sample foods from different countries

4. Healthy Food Party—Everyone brings one healthy dish

5. Chocolate Party—No explanation needed

Alisa and her friends have cake parties. "Meghan and I go over to Tiffany's house. The first thing we do is brainstorm to see what kind of cake, cookies, or muffins, or whatever that we want to make. Then Tiffany's mom takes us to the store, and we get our supplies. Then we go home and get started. We bake cakes and stuff and watch movies and eat everything we can find in the fridge. Now Meghan is a big chocolate lover. She always wants to have all chocolate stuff. Well, she persuaded me and Tiffany to make her some chocolate cake while she was baking cookies. Tiffany and I got the cake mix and made it, but it never made it to the cake pan. Tiffany and I just ate it right out of the bowl. By the time Meghan noticed, there wasn't much left. She was so mad. So she decided that she was gonna take some pudding out of the refrigerator and put it on our faces. Well, as you can imagine, this turned into an all-out war! When Tiffany's mom came downstairs and saw the mess, she immediately turned our cake party into a cleaning party. That was the last time we ever decided to have a pudding war."

However, food is not always the source of pleasure. Having an unhealthy relationship with food is all too common among young women. Having a true friend around for support can help us face and work to overcome a serious food issue.

Alex's friend is helping her through treatment for an eating disorder. "When I started having my eating disorder, it didn't seem strange to me. Other people just thought I was on a diet, and nobody really thought too much of it. My friends said things like, 'You are always on that stupid diet.' But Miranda knew something was really wrong. She did all of this research on the Internet to learn about what might be happening with me. She brought the information to my parents without me knowing about it. When they sat down to talk to me, at first I was really made at Miranda for telling them. But after a while, I realized she was only doing what she knew she had to and it was only to help me. We talked about it, and she asked me how she could help me but didn't put any pressure on me. She is trying to help me work through the problems I have. She really listens.

"When I went into treatment she came to visit me when they let me have friends. She brought me a magazine and a stuffed koala. When I opened the magazine I saw she had written all over the pages with the really skinny models. On one page she wrote: 'Help! I can't hold my head up cuz my body is too thin!' and on another she wrote: 'Don't try this at home! Dangerous to your health.' It made me laugh during a really rough time. I still haven't gotten complete control over my eating disorder, but Miranda is definitely helping me get better."

The Comforts of Home

You don't need to go anywhere to have fun with your friends. Angel e-mails: "I love to just hang out at home with them and talk about our favorite subject: Boys! :)" One of the first tentative steps toward a new friendship is to invite someone over to our house. What happens without the distractions — of teachers, classmates, the mall, the sports game — can reveal whether we can truly be friends. Some of our closest moments with our friends happen in the comfort of our own homes.

"Most of our get-togethers are at somebody's house," says Jilli. "My friends and I have each other over to play board games, do crafts, or just hang out." Amelia and her friend Roxana don't need to leave the house to enjoy each other's company. "When I'm with Roxana at home, we usually get very creative. We'll write stories together, think up whole worlds with their own special cultures and life forms, and act them out with our stuffed animals. We love to talk about our favorite books and use the computer together." Marianna says that one of the best parts of her weekend is when she and her friends all head back to somebody's house. "Marina's house is the best. We talk over coffee. Our talks are really interesting because they allow us to open up and share our feelings about things that bother us. We listen to each other's problems, help each other feel better, and try to come up with a logical solution to them. It is almost like we are taking a vacation from our daily lives."

Another way to take a mini-vacation from life is to veg out at home in front of the television. Many of the girls agreed: watching TV with a friend is much more fun than watching alone. You laugh together, cry together, and scream in fear together. "My friends and I watch TV and videos," Sydney tells us, "and then recite the lines over and over, still laughing even after a month! It's a lot of fun when you do have jokes because then you don't feel alone." Nikole and her friends watch TV together regularly. "One of our obsessions is the WB TV shows! We can never miss a show. If we know we are going to miss an episode of any show, we tape the show—not once but twice! We are obsessive TV show freaks!"

Joy says she and Elaine have rented so many movies and watched them at home "we've actually lost count of how many movies we've seen. And when we watch them, we sit next to each other, and I stick my feet underneath her to keep them warm. That's weird, but I always do it and she always complains, but I never move my feet. I've always liked how I never had to move my feet. It was just another sign of how close we are."

Isabel and her friend have discovered a movie that they feel relates to their own friendship. "We rent one movie, *Foxfire*, because it reminds us about our friendships. It is about girls who think they could never be friends, because they are all completely different. But they become friends for life, just like us: Michaela with the butler, live-in maid, and chef, Brooke who is poor, and me, with an ordinary family life. When people look at us they would think we wouldn't be friends at all."

Jessica R's Five Favorite Videos about Friendship

1. *Now and Then*
2. *Girl, Interrupted*
3. *Brokendown Palace*
4. *My Best Friend's Wedding*
5. *The Craft*

Jennifer tells how she felt Ash's trust in her become solid at a surprising, and bittersweet, moment while they were watching TV together at her house. "Ash had just moved to our school district at the beginning of seventh, and we had been hanging around together more and more. We were watching some trashy talk show about fathers who had abused their children. I was about to make fun of one of the guests when I noticed Ash was silently crying huge tears. She buried herself under my fleece blanket so I couldn't really see her face. She told me that she had lied to me about her father, who she had said had died when she was little. He really had molested her and when she finally told her mother, her mother had taken her away one night and moved to our town. Ash wasn't even her real name. She begged me not to tell anyone, and when I didn't, she knew she could really trust me. She also said she didn't know how long she would be staying in our town, but she would consider me a true friend forever. She practically lived at my house for months, but then moved away suddenly at the end of the school year. I don't know where she moved to, but I think of her often. I take comfort in the fact that maybe, even briefly, I was able to provide some stability in what was obviously a turbulent life."

Being home puts us immediately at ease. We are on our own turf, have no one to impress, and are surrounded by everything that makes us comfortable. Sometimes, like Jennifer's girlfriend, our home away from home is what brings us peace of mind.

In Harmony

Music is humanity's universal language, speaking volumes about emotion, instincts, and culture. We relate to our friends through music in many ways. Music creates an instant community with other listeners. Music can say what we cannot express in words ourselves. Uninhibited with our friends, we sing at the top of our lungs and dance around the room. We dedicate songs on the radio to our friend to tell her how much she means to us.

"Music is so important to me," Zoe tells us. "My friend Janet and I make up music videos to our CDs in our rooms together. We go to concerts all the time, and we talk about music all the time. And we sing in the hallways at school. We have been to so many concerts and we buy each other CDs and dance around and listen to the radio in the car." "I have a great passion for music," says Paige. "I love to play the piano, the guitar, and to sing and listen to music. My good friend Rachel also enjoys music and is a wonderful pianist. We have certain songs we can't wait to hear each other play again."

Jennifer and her friends were under pressure during finals week, when a little music made all the difference. "Delia and I were incredibly stressed out about our exams. We had been studying all week and were at her house preparing for our last test. You could tell we were about to crack. We were arguing and getting on each other's nerves over the stupidest things. All of a sudden, she put in a Destiny's Child CD and blasted it really loud. She assigned us parts and started lip synching all over the place. We all got in on the act. She had her stuffed lion be Beyoncé. We went nuts for a couple songs until we were exhausted from laughing so hard. When we got back to studying, we had let off steam and felt so much better."

Brittany and her friend Erica dream of being famous music artists themselves someday. "We have a band, but we haven't come up with a name we like yet though," Brittany e-mails. "So far, the best one is Storm. We have seen so many members come and go and had so many names, but we have always stayed in the band. Someday we'll make it. Erica + Brittany = Future Singers, but for now, BFF." Perhaps BFF should be the name of the band?

 Brittany's Top Five Favorite Songs about Friendship

1. "Best Friend" – Brandy
2. "Count on Me" – Whitney Houston
3. "That's What Friends Are For" – Dionne Warwick
4. "Lean on Me" – various performers
5. "For You I Will" – Monica

Katie takes her singing out on the town but doesn't have any illusions about future fame. "My friends and I all love to sing karaoke. One time we were singing karaoke at a club. I forget what song we were singing. We were purposely singing it really bad, but then I noticed the guy I liked was in the audience. If that wasn't embarrassing enough, my friend then noticed that I noticed him. She starts to sing the song, 'I Will Always Love You.' But instead of 'I' she sang '*she* will always love you,' and was pointing to me and looking right at him. It was embarrassing. But funny."

Several girls responded that one of their favorite times with a friend was going to see a favorite band. "Lizzy's and my favorite band is Hanson. We try to write songs as good as theirs, but ours aren't even close," says Elizabeth.

One of my best memories is a Hanson concert we went to in Connecticut, and we showed up without any tickets and ended up getting great seats for $5 less than the original price from a scalper. It was such a fun night!"

Sarah's friend Susan knew she had a passion for the band 'NSync, but Sarah wasn't expecting this surprise from her friend. "I really like 'NSync, and I had been trying to get tickets to their concert forever but I couldn't get them. I was sitting at home, being very bored, when my phone rang. When I answered, it was Susan, and she was like 'Guess what?' I said, 'What?' Then she paused and said, *We Are Going To The 'NSync Concert!!!* Happy birthday!' It was the best present in the world a person could give me."

Joy and her friend experienced a magical moment of true bonding at a concert, despite earlier disagreements. "Elaine and I love Ani DiFranco. We would drive around in her car and blast Ani music. We would always talk about how great she must be in concert and how much we wanted to see her perform. We taped a couple live things she did on TV and watched them, and we practically drooled. We got tickets to an Ani concert near Philadelphia. We got there way early so we decided to go into Philly to eat. On the way back, we got totally lost. We were driving around Philly going nowhere, and we started fighting. Then we made it to the concert and had the greatest time. When Ani came out on stage, the whole place went nuts. Elaine and I just looked at each other and then back at the stage and started screaming. This was something we had been waiting for for so long. We danced, and we were just in awe of Ani who is just such an amazing musician and an amazing woman. We were in our own little worlds. I remember looking over at Elaine while she was dancing and thinking how different she looked. Then Ani sang 'Two Little Girls.' We hadn't been really paying attention to each other, but when that song came on I started bawling. Elaine and I put our arms around each other and cried together. We hadn't had the best day together, getting lost in Philly and the fights that followed, but the music made us remember our friendship and what we have been through together. It was a spiritual moment."

Listening to music helps us express our deepest thoughts and emotions. Name an emotion and there is a song to reflect the way we feel. The music we listen to provides a release as we laugh, cry, or let our anger go. While listening to music can be a highly personal activity, it also is one that can be shared. When we drop the personal headphones and crank up the music, our girlfriends can take a rare peek into our true heart of hearts . . . where the music is.

Road Trips

It represents freedom. Spontaneity. The ability to escape. It is the object we can't wait to have all to ourselves. It is The Car. But before we can take off down the road, of course, we have to learn how to drive. While some of us learn with our parents cowering in the passenger seat, others share learning to drive as a group experience: in driver's ed. Megan and her friend Alli took driver's ed class together. "We happened to get put in the same class, so we were able to do our driving time together. We had a blast driving together, making jokes about how horrible we both were. One time she was going to switch lanes, and she thought that by looking in her side mirrors she could tell if anyone was there. She looked and didn't see anyone so she started changing lanes. Both the teacher and I screamed out in alarm when we noticed a car right beside us who had been in her blind spot. She hadn't learned about the blind spot yet. We barely missed hitting the car. Surprisingly we got through our class without wrecking or damaging any cars."

Brittany and her friend are getting their practice in now to, hopefully, avoid those situations. "Whenever I go to an amusement park with a friend, we go on the bumper cars. We pretend we are taking our driver's test, but someone always hits us. Then we get angry and chase after them, so I guess in real life we'll fail."

Trinity got her permit last year and went driving with her mother and her friend Kat. "Driving home, I ran through a stop sign. This was not the rolling stop Philadelphia drivers are notorious for, where you slow down but don't stop. This was full speed ahead. My mom was freaking out, so I pulled over but when I did I ran over the curb twice. So I've been deemed by both Kat and my mom that I deserve only to drive in Philly. Driving in Philly is like driving in New York City, only ten times harder and more dangerous!"

Then we pass the driver's test. The keys to the car are in our hands, and we wave good-bye to our parents. We are free. One of the first things we do, of course, is drive straight to our friend's house and tell her to jump in. Ami's friends had to suffer through her new driving skills, or lack of them. "I just got my permit, and one day I was driving Kathryn and Aggie home, and I missed a turn. I knew the road really well; it's one of the main drags in the town I've lived in my entire life. So I missed this turn, and I went into my school stadium, and was doing a massive U-turn, and Kathryn went insane, screaming about how she got carsick. Kat was literally turning green. Finally I got her home, and I think she really did get ill because she was absent the next day! However, she always wants rides home, so I don't think she was too traumatized."

Having a license does not always mean we know where we are going. Patricia tells us, "Whenever my two other friends and I go out somewhere in a car we always, no matter what, get lost somewhere. We can even get lost in our hometown. It's just crazy that we can get lost anywhere. And of course, we were once in the middle of nowhere, and our car broke down. We were stranded for two hours until someone came and fixed it."

Marianna's Dream Road Trip Cross-Country with Her Friends

1. Mountain climbing in the Adirondacks
2. South Beach, Florida, to dance with gorgeous guys
3. Dude ranch in Houston, Texas, to live as cowgirls for a few days
4. Get rich at some casinos in Las Vegas
5. Get celebrity autographs in Los Angeles

Sydney tells us this story. "It seems that a lot of people seem to have staring problems whenever me and my friends are out on the road. One day we were coming home from school and were stopped at a red light next to a school bus packed with annoying kids. I had brought home a large protester's sign from a play, and it simply read Stop It! We finally got fed up with the gestures so I opened the sun roof and held up the sign, and they all looked and laughed. My friend Keely (the driver and owner of the car) thought it was so great so I made her a slightly smaller sign to use whenever people stare . . . and we do. We also made up another sign that says Take a Picture — It Lasts Longer for those who stare.

Once we get our driver's license, we are off. For a while some of us are allowed to drive only in the neighborhood. Others take major road trips. Aviva got to hit the beach with her friend Katherine over the summer. "We grew very close during the trip. We had to share a room, and we'd spend the night just talking and listening to the sounds of the ocean, from like 1:00 A.M. until at least 4:00 A.M. We talked a lot about the beach boys we met during the day."

Corin and her friends had a road trip to remember, when they were just relieved to get there. "One time, over spring break last year, my friends went to visit our friend Amy in York, Pennsylvania, which she told us was only one hour away. Well, it was four hours away. Seven of us packed into my station wagon, and it started to rain. The thing was, my windshield wipers weren't working, and no one in PA uses their headlights. I was going about five miles per hour on a major highway, and Alex was sitting in the passenger seat with her head out the window, trying to read the road signs so we knew where we were."

Being on the road also involves a lot of responsibility. Sometimes it takes courage to recognize when someone shouldn't be driving and to stand up to do the right thing.

"Friends don't let friends drive drunk," the saying goes. Trinity shares this story. "I was at a party. My friend Kelly had drunk a lot, but she wanted to drive home. I took her keys and hid them in one of the bedrooms. Kelly got pissed off because she wanted to leave, and she started breaking things. But we made her calm down and then get in the car with me instead."

"You are never more popular than the day you get your driver's license," someone once said. When we pile into the car with our friends, we never know what adventure will be ahead of us. And when we arrive safely at our destination, our friends can let out a big sigh of relief.

Cementing
the Bonds

As we listen to each other and learn to trust our girlfriends, our relationships become stronger. Sharing our innermost thoughts and feelings connects us at the deepest level of our beings. And if fate should part us from our girlfriends, we stay connected to each other through all our beloved memories.

Hearing Each Other

One of the most important things our friends can ever do for us is to just listen to us. Whether we are sad, frustrated, furious, or, let's face it, semi-irrational, having a friend listen to us can help lighten the load. "Listening, not imitation, may be the sincerest form of flattery," psychologist Dr. Joyce Brothers once said. When a friend really listens, you know that she really cares.

We talk to connect with each other. What we say might be everyday stuff, but it helps us to learn about each other, to bond with each other, to reassure each other that our thoughts and feelings are OK.

Our friends help us to work through our everyday problems and process our thoughts. Nothing is too inconsequential to be discussed. Sometimes our conversations are just our stream of consciousness, but as we babble to our friends, we can sort out our real feelings. Katie and her friends talk nonstop about anything and everything. "My friends and I talk about everything, like grades, homework, boys, dances, hair, clothes, family things, etc. Whatever happens to be on our minds then. My friends are the type where you can tell them anything, and in some way or another they can relate." "Mary, SFunk, AT, and I talk about everything under the sun," says Katie Lou. "We talk about politics, clothes, our families, boys, writing, sex, school, and really weird topics that are better left unmentioned."

We all know that friends are great for giving advice, but sometimes all we really need is just for someone we trust to listen to us. Nikole calls listening the best gift a friend can give. "The best thing that a friend has done for me was to listen. She would never speak, never lecture, never give advice unless asked, never reprimand, never badger. The only thing she would do was listen to what I said, and sometimes what I never said. The thing I love the most is to be able to not speak yet have a conversation. Friendships are strength that way." With all of the frustrations that accompany our teen years, having a friend who will put up with our venting can help get it all out of our systems so we can move on.

"If I'm feeling sad or depressed or desperate to talk about something, my friends are the people I go to," says Jessica R. "A friend who not only listens to you, but really *hears* you, is the only kind of friend worth having. Sometimes, all I need to do is tell someone about my day, whether it was good or bad. I just need someone to listen and give me feedback or advice. I feel so lucky to know that I can just call my friends and spill everything to them, and they'll be there to give me their opinion. My friends are like my own personal therapists, and I am theirs."

Morgan recognizes the importance of listening. "I had this one friend who would go on and on for hours talking all about herself. I didn't have a chance to get a word in. When I said something, she would steer the conversation back to herself. I realized that I couldn't let a friendship go on like that, because she didn't care what I thought or wanted to say. It was totally one-sided. I told her I thought our friendship would be better if she could listen to me talk, too. She said OK but after a few days was back to her old self, going on and on. I had to stop being friends with her. Listening is so important to a friendship—but *both* of you have to listen to each other!"

Marianna tells us about her listening friend. "I have only one special friend who listens to my everyday chat and never gets tired of me. Marina always listens to my troubles and a lot of minor stuff, and offers very useful advice for which I'm very grateful. Sometimes I don't want to burden people with my minor issues. With Marina, it's different; I never even once felt like I have bothered her by telling her my feelings. I guess it's because she shares so much of her own personal stuff with me. We listen a lot to each other and help to cope with the challenging issues of everyday life. Her listening helps me a lot, because it allows me to feel cared for. It lets me know I'm not alone and that someone out there is hearing what I've got to say."

One of the best things about having a girlfriend is knowing that you have someone you can turn to when you need to talk. Whether we just need to get little annoyances off our chests or we have a major crisis and need to talk for hours, we know our girlfriends will be there with attentive ears, open minds, and caring hearts. And we'll clear our schedules at the drop of a hat if our girlfriends need us to listen for a while.

What We Talk About

1. Clothes — what to wear to school, and, more importantly, what not to wear

2. School — homework, grades, tests, teachers we love, and teachers we love to hate

3. Guys — crushes, hotties, boyfriends, and just friends

4. Families — the good, the bad, and the ugly

5. Sex — the reliable and not so reliable scoop

6. Celebrities — who's on our hot lists and hit lists

7. Activities — places to go, people to see, plans for the weekend

8. Movies, music, and books — what to see, what to hear, and what to read

9. Hair and makeup — from the good days to the put-a-bag-over-our-head days

10. Other people — we just can't resist that gossip

Sharing Confidences

We all have secrets, things we cannot imagine telling anyone but our best girlfriends. Perhaps we have done something that does not make us proud. Maybe we have a thought that we need to share, and we just have to tell someone. And let's face it, we all have secret crushes sometimes—and though it's no fun if we don't share it with someone, we don't want it to become common knowledge either. It works the other way too; when a girlfriend trusts us enough to tell us a secret, we feel honored to have the privilege of her faith in us.

According to Allison, friends are crucial because "you have to have someone that you can tell all your secrets to. A diary is great, of course, but a diary doesn't give you advice. It doesn't tell you whether it thinks the guy down the street is cute. If I didn't have friends to talk to about things, I would go insane. My secrets might be anything from a huge crisis in my life to the latest gossip about the head cheerleader."

Knowing that you can trust a girlfriend to keep a secret puts that friendship in a special place in your heart. "I can tell Tiffany *anything,* and I know that she won't tell anyone any of my secrets," says Melissa. "But that's also partly because she knows that if she does tell anyone, I could easily get her back. I won't say anything, but let's just say she's done some pretty bad Truth or Dares." Joy and her best friend have shared secrets and know they can completely trust each other. "One time, Elaine told me she had this deep, deep secret that she couldn't tell anyone. And then one night I told her my deepest, deepest secret, and it turned out to be the same as hers! The secret was one of those things that if your other friends found out, they'd probably never talk to you again. That's probably the biggest time I confided in her. There have been numerous times after that, too many to say, but she has never once judged me, and I know I can always go to her when I have a problem, no matter what it is. I can trust her."

Isabel and her friend Kayley have secret wish boxes. "They are plaster boxes that we decorated with beads. Mine is purple, hers is pink. We write down our secret wishes and put them in the box. When we go to each other's house, we read what each has written. Then we try to help each other make a plan to get them. We don't share our wish boxes with anyone else."

Katie knew when her friend didn't reveal a confidence, she qualified as a girlfriend. "One time I told my friend a secret about my family. I was a little worried she would tell, since it was something really important. We soon got into an argument and I thought for sure she would tell then, but she didn't. Even when we were in a fight, she never told. Now I don't regret telling her my secret because I know she is a good enough friend to never tell no matter how big a fight we ever get into."

Gabriela has learned the hard way how important it is to keep secrets. "A big mistake that I made in the past was telling someone a secret that was supposed to be kept confidential. At one time it was hard for me to keep a really good secret, especially if the secret was about someone I knew. But as I grew older, I began to think of secrets as being sacred promises to my friends."

When we share our confidences with a girlfriend, or when she trusts us with a secret, a new bond forms between us. This bond is like a single strand of silk from a spider's web, growing stronger and stronger with each day the secret is kept. And then, when the web is woven, we know who our true friends are.

 ## Nikole's Five Things You Can Tell Your Best Friend

1. Your parents are getting a divorce (you tell her right after you find out)

2. You like the "nerdy" guy

3. You still have your New Kids On The Block cassette tape

4. All about your first kiss

5. He really dumped you—not the other way around

Keeping in Touch

Ring, beep, that little bell when an instant message pops up on your screen. Each of these familiar sounds brings the promise of a connection with a friend. We keep in touch with our friends by phone, our pagers, and online. When we can't be in the same room we at least know that when we need them, we can reach out and find our friends. What is the object most used by, most coveted by, most associated with teen girls? The phone, of course. We are notorious phone hogs. Woe to the family that doesn't have more than one line. Anyone expecting to call that house should expect to hear a busy signal, or at the least a call waiting click. Our parents complain we will have to have the phone surgically removed from our ear, we are on it so much. But the phone provides a connection to each other that is both physical and emotional. We know that whenever we need them, our friends are only a few dialed digits away.

Melissa and her friend are avowed phoneaholics. "We talk practically every day! For an hour at least! We are always hogging the phone lines and our parents and siblings get pretty mad at us, but we just have to do it!" Jamie talked to her friend Liz so much her mother quickly gave in to her request for her own phone. "We talk for about half an hour or an hour every day, but sometimes it's just us both doing homework and watching TV without saying a whole lot. I have my own phone line, which my mom got me in the sixth grade. I use it *all* the time. Liz and I would always try to break our record for staying up late talking and sometimes would try falling asleep with the phone still on until one of our phones would start beeping from a low battery, and we'd hang up."

Now that cell phones and beepers are common among teens, it is possible to stay in touch anywhere, anytime. Melissa and her friends have a system worked out on their beepers. "I beep my friends to say hi to them in code. 14 means hi (turn the pager upside down and it looks like h-i). 411 means I have gossip. 0–0 means something's wrong so call me — get it? Oh-oh."

Joy has discovered the joy of cell phones. She tells us, "I moved recently, and my best friend actually got a cell phone so we could talk to one another long distance and not have any phone charges. The phone keeps me close with all my friends. So many of them live far enough away that it costs money to call them, but we do it anyway. When you can't be with your friends, you can at least talk to them. It makes the humdrum routine of your house less humdrum and routine. Elaine and I talk on our cell phones because it ends up being cheaper. It helps keep our conversations short because our cell phones always end up running out of power."

When we are not talking to each other, we are writing each other. Sometimes our written messages are brief and to the point. "Friday. Mall. Six o'clock. Be there." The most common form of written communication between teen girls? "It has to be notes," Nikole laughs. "The dread of teachers everywhere! There have been many notes passed between my friends and me. I've tried to keep most, and it's funny to go back and read what was going on two years ago. To my surprise, I have never been caught (knock on wood)!"

 Jessica's Top Five Ways to Communicate with Our Girlfriends

1.	In person
2.	Via phone
3.	Online
4.	Notes passed in class
5.	Psychic messages

Allison and her friend Kenleigh have an elaborate note-passing system. "In school, we write notes to each other. If we're in the same class, one of us will write a note and go 'sharpen her pencil,' leaving the folded-up note behind the machine. A couple minutes later, the other person will go to sharpen her pencil and retrieve the note.

Allison tells us how she and her friends keep in touch with each other. "My best friends and I have this blue, leopard print notebook that we pass around at school. We use Sarah's locker as a mailbox, and we all write group notes in there. The idea actually originated from a note-book that Kate and I started, but then Taylor and Sarah joined the group, so we got a bigger notebook. It makes for some interesting notes. There are word searches, crossword puzzles, connect the dots . . . everything." Katie Lou and her friend also passed a notebook back and forth. "In eighth and ninth grade, SFunk and I kept a run-ning notebook full of our notes called the Note-Notebook. It almost got intercepted like a million times, but we man-aged to always keep it away from the teachers. Notebooks really helped us to keep in touch, especially during ninth grade because we didn't have any classes together. We both have the bad habit of interrupting one another when we're talking, and the notebooks really helped us to get it all out with zero interruptions. It also made it easier to talk about things that perhaps we'd feel more uncomfort-able talking about in person. They were basically just a lot of babbling, silly poems, goofy cartoons, and raunchy jokes. We also gossiped about other people a lot, etc. So mean! I have both of them now, and it's great to go back and relive those times."

❀   ❀   ❀

Chatting through the computer is the most modern way to exchange notes. Not only can we save the conversations to reread later, we can share intimate secrets, or even tell our friend's pesky little brother to get off the computer and stop hogging the one phone line so we can call our girlfriend. Many girls told us they sit down at their computers at home and e-mail away to friends who live nearby. "I could pick up the phone, I suppose, and I often do. But I also e-mail and Instant Message the girls in my class. From 'What are you wearing tomorrow?' to 'I have a serious problem.'" Reasons to chat online versus talking on the phone include being able to leave messages for others who aren't able to be there, to look like you are doing homework when you are really chatting, to send your thoughts to many people at once, and to disclose without having to see the person's face or even hear their reaction. "My friend Monet lives only a street away so I could just run over there," says Jenny. "But for some reason, as soon as I come home from school we get on the computer and Instant Message each other. We IM about a boy she really likes, and she will go on about him for hours. And if one of us can't be on, we will write long e-mails to make up for it, and the other can read them later. I usually IM my friends because it is more convenient than calling. I like instant messaging because it allows me to talk to as many people as I want to at one time, whereas calling someone is usually limited to one person."

Whether we communicate by mouth or by hand, whether we write our thoughts on scraps of paper or on the computer screen, our words connect us to each other. We'll always remember passing notes, sending e-mails, and talking with our best of girlfriends; it gives us access to each other's heart and deepest feelings. Communication gives us the truth about our girlfriends.

Lifesavers

During our most troubled times, just knowing someone is there to listen to us can bring us comfort. When we face serious problems, our friends can help us sort out our confusion. They can share a new perspective and give us much-needed advice when our own heads might not be so clear.

Angel's friend helped her get through a rough time when her parents were going through a divorce. "I leaned on my friend, and she didn't let me fall. She prayed for me and just told me that if I ever needed a friend to talk to she was there. She also seemed to sense when I needed a hug and when I wasn't OK even if I said I was OK. She was a wonderful friend during that time of my life. And she still is." Joanne couldn't stop agonizing over something that had been said to her until she confided in her friend Lisa. "A supposed friend said awful things about how my birth parents, who had put me up for adoption because they couldn't afford a third child, had 'thrown me away.' She also made rude comments about my foster parents. It felt good to be able to talk to Lisa about something which, to me, was terribly painful."

Serious Issues We Discuss with Our Friends

1. Eating disorders
2. Divorce
3. Alcohol
4. Drugs
5. Sex
6. Pregnancy
7. Illness
8. Suicide
9. Death

Janessa tells about a time when she helped her friend see that running from problems does not solve them. "My friend Rebecca called me one night around 6:30. She told me about another fight she and her mom had had. She told me that she was going to run away from there the next day and not tell her mom where she was going. I told her that she better not because there were lots of consequences to think about. I guess she thought about what I had said because it worked and she didn't run away."

Our friends are there for us, whether it is through a long, difficult time like Angel, or just a night of raging emotions and confusion. "Even just tonight, I felt like I was about to have a mental breakdown," Kathlynn describes. "But my best friend was there for me. I talked to her about everything that was going on in my life, and I felt better. I am PMSing and having guy problems at the same time. I slept with my boyfriend, and now I am thinking he wants to break up with me. It is a bad night. But she is helping me learn from my mistakes."

Even just listening to a friend can help in dramatic ways. Sometimes we recognize that a friend is in serious trouble, and although we know we cannot save her from that trouble, we help her find someone trusted who can see her through the hardest moments in life. Kerri tells us how just listening to a friend can help in life-altering ways. "I had a friend who told me she had just tried to kill herself by swallowing twenty-five aspirin. I knew it wasn't enough to kill her, but I also knew it was a cry for help. So my other friend she told and I told a teacher, who told a counselor, who told her parents. They took her to the emergency room, but she was OK. At first she was mad that we told because she thought her mom would be mad at her. But now she is much better and happier that we did what we needed to do."

Trinity has a friend who needed a caring listener at the lowest part of her life. "My friend Laura is stuck in a really bad life. Her parents are always fighting, and she feels that she is unlovable. She saw the marks on my wrists from when I tried to commit suicide a few years ago. She started asking me questions, like how to cut the skin right so you bleed to death. I knew then she was suicidal and she needed to get help. And I helped her get it right away."

When a friend provides a listening ear, we are one step closer to figuring it all out. We gain a new perspective from her advice or her words of support. We work through the thoughts and confusion, and release our innermost feelings that we have locked away inside ourselves. A friend who provides a listening ear is our lifeline to understanding ourselves and making ourselves better friends and better people.

Letting Us Down

When a friend betrays us, we can feel a pain as sharp as any we have felt before. We believe we can trust a friend, and suddenly she breaks our faith. Some of these betrayals are short-lived, and a friend's apology might be all that is needed for us to forgive our friend and make peace. Brooke forgave her friend's betrayal because "she quickly came to her senses. One of my friends ditched me to be popular for a few months. But then when they had used her and abused her, she came crawling back to me and asked for forgiveness. And of course, being the nice person I am, I said yes."

If a foundation of friendship is trust, our friends have certainly made cracks in the foundation at times. Sometimes the betrayal is minor, and the damage can be repaired. Katanaya's story shows how even a small lie isn't worth the potential harm to a friendship. "One time my best friend didn't want to hang out with me so she lied and said her parents weren't letting her go out that night. Then she had her dad come and fake yell at her to make it seem real. She later confessed she had been lying. She apologized and we got over it, but it still hurt a little. But it just seems ridiculous; she got her dad into it! She could have just told me she felt like staying home! I let it go — this time."

When we betray our friends, we can only hope they will find it in their hearts to forgive us. Jilli shares this story. "My friend was having family problems and she told one of our classmates in confidence. I heard the classmate telling some other girls about it and then everyone knew. The girl who blabbed it felt really bad. We have a tradition that when one of us does something that makes another person feel bad, we write a note to apologize. She wrote a note to my friend saying she was so sorry. My friend wrote her a note back saying she felt better because of the apology. So everyone forgave each other." But other times we can't make it up to our friend, no matter how hard we try.

The cut is too deep, and an apology isn't enough to cover the wound.

Angel admits she can not fully trust her friends who betrayed her. "I had several of my friends betray me once, and to this day I cannot understand why they did. All of a sudden there were all these rumors flying around about me at school, saying I was this and that and I did this and that. It really hurt me. It destroyed some friendships, but I ended up making up with some of the people involved. It was hard. We never really spoke about it; we just kinda started over. Forgive and forget, in a way. But I am not sure if it will ever be the same because I will always have this feeling like they might be thinking of betraying me again."

"I turned my back on my friend Bridget when some new friends came along," says Alisa. "I wouldn't hang out with her anymore; I was always too busy. Now we don't really talk anymore because she got tired of waiting for me to come around. I realized I was wrong, but it was too late. If I could do things differently, I would have made more time for her from the beginning so we would still be friends today."

Some betrayals can destroy a friendship permanently. Sometimes a small betrayal tells us that this is a friend who does not truly care about us. Melissa describes her friend's betrayal: "I really liked this guy and told her about him. At lunch, she said she was going to go over and ask him out for me. But she asked him out for herself, instead. She came back and told me that he was going to go out with her. I was so upset and she said to me, 'He never would have liked you anyway.'"

 Katie's List of Five Things That Can Break Up a Friendship

1. Lying

2. Breaking promises

3. Spreading rumors

4. Going out with the other's ex

5. Drifting apart and making new friends who replace you

Some friends continue to betray us time after time. We eventually learn we just can't count on these friends. No matter how much we want to believe that they love us and just made a mistake, we will continue to be disappointed until we finally realize that they are not good friends for us. These friends must be placed in our ex files. Trinity's friend broke her word one too many times. She mourns this friendship lost through betrayal: "Friends are supposed to be your second family. When no one else is there for you, your friend is supposed to be. Well, one day, that ceases to exist and the world as you once knew it ceases to exist. All the stability you ever knew becomes a jumble of instability and confusion; any sense of security you ever felt in this insecure world has vanished, never to reappear. The false sense of hope that you are tightly holding onto is slowly slipping away, your fingers becoming intertwined with the sharp needle-like point of a barbed wire suit, which you will soon wear as a punishment. A punishment for all the times you let yourself be fooled by your 'friends' and let yourself be hurt, over and over again. Now you are wearing the tight armor of pain you have brought on yourself, which will not be released until you have forgiven yourself for all the pain you have brought them and they have brought you."

Being betrayed by a friend can be devastating, but it's a part of reality almost all of us experience at one time. Betrayal can teach us valuable lessons. "From the inevitable hurts and rejections typical of this period, teens also learn how to be more discriminating in their friendships and how to discern true friends from false friends," wrote Dr. Carol J. Eagle and Carol Colman, in *All That She Can Be*.[3] We learn to watch for warning signs in the future, to forgive when we should and to move forward when we shouldn't. And, we learn to hold fast to the true friends we really do have.

Separations

It may seem like we are so close nothing can break us apart. And then, one of our friends announces that she is moving. Whether it is a move across town or a move across the world, distance changes friendships. On the surface, it might seem practical to just let these friendships go. Now you can't hang out in your room after school, you don't have the same people in common to talk about, and those long-distance phone charges add up. But we hold on tight to our true friends and don't let distance get in the way.

Laura still feels the pain of separation from her friend Brittany. "Brittany only moved about an hour and a half away but, still, it hurt. We only get to see each other about twice a year, and we talk about every other month over the Internet. I really do miss her a lot, and I feel we just aren't as close any more. But no matter how far apart we are, she will always be close in my heart."

"My friend Angelica moved when we were seven," Jenny says. "We said we would write or keep in touch, but we didn't. Four years later, out of the blue, a package arrived in the mail. It was from Angelica! She wrote in a letter that she wanted me to have something to remember her by and make sure I was still thinking of her today. And she sent a beaded frog she had made for me. I still have it today."

Mandy has experienced the separation of moving, but she hasn't left her friends behind. Nor have they left her. "I moved to a different town so I don't get to see my old friends too much. But the night my parents told me they were separating I was really upset. I called Marisela crying. She called our other friend Tara, and within a few hours Tara's mom had driven them out to see me."

"Randi was one of my closest homeschooling friends," says Stephanie. "She moved six thousand miles away to Hawaii. It was very hard for all of my homeschooling friends when she moved. Randi was the only homeschooler who lived near me. Just this past year we had started taking the train to each other's house to save our parents from driving. Not only did that make us feel more independent, but we also got to spend a lot more time together. Her parents wanted to move and she didn't, so it was a very hard move for her. It was at a confusing time in a teenage girl's life, when you tend to really need your friends and when it's hard to make new ones. She was like my second family, and I was with her at least two times a week, if not more. I felt so comfortable around her because we could have a goofy conversation about a boy or a deep conversation about something that was bothering us. She was the first friend I cried with, and I will always remember that. I miss her so much and every time I talk to her and hear how unhappy she is there, I miss her even more. I know I have to go on with my life and that eventually she will make new friends. We stay in touch, but it will never be the same."

Brittny's friend Sarah lives part of the year with each parent. "So she lives with her father out of state and then comes to live here with her mom. When she is at her dad's, we e-mail each other and keep in touch. When she comes back she'll call, and we'll go back to be being friends without the distance. It is sad when she has to leave again. But I try to just focus on enjoying her and having fun and appreciating when she is here."

Christine is the one who moved and still misses her friends she left behind. "My family moved to Japan, and I was so scared because I would be going to a new school on a new continent. I made a lot of really good friends while I was there, especially Laura, Elizabeth, and Charlotte. I still cry when I look at their yearbooks. It was very hard to leave friends like those."

Five Gifts to Give a Friend Who Is Moving

1. Photo album filled with pictures of you both
2. A going-away bash
3. A long-distance calling card (to call you, of course)
4. A box of stationery and stamps
5. A video of you and your other friends sharing memories

Hello, Good-bye

Sometimes we make an instant connection with a person, and we just know we'll always be friends. Summer activities often lead to these kinds of bonds: a girl at the beach asks us if we want to swim with her, we meet a whole new set of friends at camp, or the neighbors have their granddaughter visit for two weeks and we are introduced to one another. It's amazing how we develop bonds with people we only see for a short time.

Britt stays close to friends she knows from a summer camp in New York. "I have been going there since I was six," she says, "and I love all my friends there. It's cool because you meet people from all over the country, and you cherish time with them more because you only see them once a year." Rosemary sees her friend just twice a year, but each time they are together it is as if no time has passed at all. "Twice a year, the people in the same youth groups in nearby states come together for an amazing event called Y.O.U. Rally. The people at rally are my special occasion friends. To be able to spend three to five days with three hundred angels, apart from the outside world and in a place that is just love, plain and simple, is the most wonderful experience you can imagine. We are one, we are unity for that time. Even though I only see these people eight days a year, I am extremely close to a lot of them. We keep in touch by e-mail and phone. I could tell any of them anything, even if I had never met them before. That's how amazing they are."

 Top Five Places We Make Fleeting Friends

1. Summer camp
2. Vacations
3. Visits to relatives
4. Youth group trips
5. Sports competitions

Jenny tells us about an instant connection she made with her girlfriend while on a trip. "My aunt and uncle own a hotel in Florida. We were on vacation there when I was eight. I met a girl named Mallory who was staying there from Alabama. I went to the beach and hung out at the hotel with her for a week. We kept in touch writing letters and e-mails and talking on the phone. When we were ten we went to the hotel again. I got there, and my aunt said, 'Mallory is here!' It was a shock since we didn't know each other was going to be there. Then last year, she wrote she was going down with her family again, and my parents said we could go visit at the same time. We spent six days together at the beach, a water park, and on the rides. We now write to each other at least once a month and e-mail in the meantime. It's so amazing how we have only spent three weeks of our lives together, yet we can be so close."

These friends know you for a brief moment in time, often when we are not hampered by the pressures of school, grades, and our reputations. Other people at Jamie's camp carried a different perception of her, which in turn changed her perception of herself. "I spent five weeks in California with my aunt the summer before ninth grade. Because I was from halfway across the country, I was popular—something I had never been before. I was at this theater camp when I met Jeanhel. She was a gorgeous thirteen-year-old girl from the Philippines. I'd never seen anyone so exotic before, and I didn't expect that we'd ever be friends. But we shared a knack for annoying the adults at camp. She was always nice to me, which kids at home weren't, and we had *so* much fun whenever we were together. I was the loud Minnesotan who didn't know how to kiss and she was the girl who all the guys liked, but it was like we were two pieces next to each other in a puzzle. I haven't talked to my California friends much since I left, but she remains my favorite. Thoughts of her often come to me in my quest to make decisions and try something new: 'What would Jeanhel have done?'"

Though we see them only once in a while, or even see them only once, these friends make an impact on us. Like Britt and Rosemary, we might look forward to seeing them a next time. Or like Jamie, we might know we will likely never see this friend again. But for those moments in time, we can enjoy their presence and take with us the memory of the time we shared.

You've Got Mail

The Internet provides us with a way to reach millions of people with long-distance friend potential. We can instantly connect no matter where we live. When we make a new e-mail pal, or e-pal, we have a relationship that is unlike any other.

Jessica describes the advantages of e-pals. "One of the best things about having e-mail friends is that you can choose to open yourselves up completely. You don't worry they will blab your secrets to everyone at school, they aren't competing for the same guy, and they can be more objective than your best friend who is right in the middle of your fight with the other girls in your group. My e-pal and I e-mail at least twice a week and IM almost every night. I believe our friendship is so unique because even though I have never met her, she knows me better than anyone. I can tell her anything, and she won't judge me; she just gives me her advice and thoughts.

E-mail friends don't judge you on your look or what you wear. They don't judge you on whether you are in the popular clique at school. There are no external distractions. They learn about you through your thoughts, ideas, and words. Angel notes, "I think it's great that you can chat and get to know people online without meeting them first because then you aren't distracted by their looks." Nikole values the advice her e-mail friends give her because she knows it is more objective than what her friends might say to her face. "I think e-mail friends are the easiest to talk to because they can't see you or judge what you say. E-mail friends give you advice of the best kind because it is based on the real you."

Nikole has come to appreciate the world of friendship that the Internet has opened up for her. "I had a pen pal who I met through a project our schools did when we were in the third grade. We wrote letters all through the summer until some terrible news came through one of her last letters. One of her close friends had moved away so now they were going to be pen pals, and she didn't have time for two. It broke my heart! I was sad; how would I find another friend to write to? Until I discovered the Internet a few years later. What friends it held inside its endless web sites and chat rooms! I still chat with the first person I met online. Jen taught me everything I would need to know about the world of chats and web pages. Her friendship was something I'll never forget."

Katie Lou found a friend, Donna, online who shares a common passion—writing. "We were both writing separate, unrelated stories at the same time and posting them on AOL message boards for others to read. We recognized each other's talent, and when we finished our separate work, Donna suggested that we cowrite. We wrote a story called 'No More Us' that got a lot of comments and praise, and currently we are writing something new called 'Rearranging.'" Katie Lou also has found an online group of friends who share something in common with her. "I belong to an online club of girls, raised in the south, who basically love *Gone with the Wind* and all else southern. Ames and I are very into it. We live in Missouri, and it's pretty much up to the person whether they are a Southerner or a Northerner. Ames and I are good Southerners, and we are incredibly proud to be G.R.I.T.S!"

Pass this on to all of your friends, even if it means sending it to the person that sent it to you. And if you receive this e-mail many times from many different people, it only means that you have many friends.

And if you get it but once, do not be discouraged for you will know that you have at least one good friend.

—Making the rounds on the Internet

Our e-mail friends can even become friends with each other and form a group. We can contribute to an e-mail chain that is sent from person to person. And thanks to instant messaging, a bunch of us can chat all at the same time. Allison is part of an e-mail clique of the best kind. "I have several e-mail friends that I talk to every day through IMs. It's unique because they can offer opinions on things without some of the bias that my other friends feel. It's funny because really, we're just like normal friends; there's a group of us and everyone's friends with everyone."

"My closest e-mail pal is Amy," Marianna tells us. "Any time we feel the need to talk to someone, we always know who to turn to—each other! She has been such a good pal and a great listener. Amy has done many special things to make me feel more happy and less depressed. She introduced me to an Interactive Youth Discussion Group. This program is designed to allow teenagers who have similar interests or problems to communicate with each other through e-mail. Throughout the time that I have been in this program, I have befriended many courageous and interesting teenagers who I now consider to be my second family. If Amy would have never introduced me to this group, I would have never met so many wonderful people. I'm very blessed to have such a great e-mail pal like her."

Occasionally we are able to meet our e-pals face to face, as Marianna did. "I met Inna on the Internet, and she lives in the same city as I do. After a while, we decided to meet up and hang out. Our parents checked things out and OK'd the plans. We had no plans, just to 'relax and just chill out' as Inna called it. We just basically walked around the boardwalk and got acquainted. Meeting Inna was a very nice experience. I got to see her face to face and find out a lot more about her character. I would wish to have met up with a lot of my e-mail pals, but unfortunately that's not really possible. I'm just very glad to have gotten the chance to do so this time."

Respecting Our Differences

Friends don't have to be alike. In fact, having friends who are different from us provides us with an incredible opportunity. These friends can expand our horizons, open us up to interests different from our own, and broaden our world. Coming from different backgrounds can give us the opportunity to observe life from a different perspective. It opens our mind and lets us open our hearts.

"I am Indian, and we have this event at my temple every year called *gurba*," says Aneri. "My best friend is white, but I take her anyway and she wears Indian clothes and joins the fun. It's so great because there is such a culture clash between us and it doesn't affect the friendship, just makes it better."

Stephanie's friends respect the differences in their religions. "When they have a Christmas party, they always remember that I am Jewish and will cross out Christmas on the invitation and write Holiday or Chanukah instead. It always touches me that they take a little extra time to remember and respect my religion. These gestures make me feel like they really care."

Brooke and her friends are open and accepting about their differences in religion and pull together to help pray for one of their friends. "Most of my friends in other religions are open to learning about other cultures and religions, just like I am. I help decorate their Christmas trees, and they come over for Shabbat and help cook and celebrate. It is great fun and a great way to learn. Right now I have a friend who is terminally ill. I pray for her and my Christian friends pray for her, and we all know that our prayers are equal and going right to God. And for my friends who don't totally understand my religion, we just don't bring it up. Religion is a deep and sensitive subject, and not all friendships can handle it. But the ones that can are strong and extra special."

Each of our families has its own traditions, values, issues, and problems. Being able to share in the culture of a girlfriend's family lets us see a whole new dimension of our friend, and we can appreciate and love her more for it. Whether we love her family or find them a bit, well, strange, we always love our girlfriend.

Isabel admits that she was not only surprised when she first visited her friend at home, but even a little intimidated. "The first time I went over to Michaela's house was the first time I realized her family was very rich. My mom drove me there, and we had to be buzzed in by a guard at the gate of a group of enormous houses. When I rang her doorbell, a butler answered it and announced me. While I was waiting for her to come down, I looked around and saw how elaborate her house was. I started to feel really awkward. I wondered, 'Do I belong here?' But then Michaela came down. She wasn't any different at home than at school. Being with her made me feel comfortable. I won't say that I am now used to the fact that the chef makes us dinner and the live-in maid cleans up after us. But I do enjoy watching videos on her huge surround-sound television and swimming in her pool. I realized that her money didn't affect our friendship at all when she came to my house, which is regularly, and she didn't seem to think twice about it. She doesn't act like she thinks she is any better than I am."

Sometimes life at a friend's house takes some getting used to. It doesn't mean that lifestyle is strange or wrong; when values and traditions are different from our own, we have a wonderful chance to learn more about our friend and celebrate our differences. "My group of homeschooled friends have very different family beliefs from mine. My friends Gabriela, Stephanie, and Randi are all *strict* vegetarians and vegans. A vegan is someone who doesn't eat any dairy or products from animals such as milk, cheese, and eggs. They also don't wear any wool or leather. I'm neither a vegetarian nor a vegan, and it took me a while to adjust to their lifestyle. Every time I go to their houses I have to eat their food, which is all soy and tofu. Their parents won't allow them to eat any sweets or junk food. In the beginning, when we first became friends, I didn't understand any of this and I thought they were strange. How can you live without sugar? I had never been around people with such strong beliefs about food! It took a while, but now I'm used to their differences. I think it's great that they're so healthy and that they care so much about animals. I admire them. But I still like to tease them sometimes, like when they sneak a candy bar or something behind their parents' backs. I'm like, 'Wow, you're such a rebel! You're so brave! If they catch you, you're done for!'"

We might even have the opportunity to explore another culture *with* our girlfriend and experience the amazement together. Jamie and her friend Nina had an incredible opportunity to travel together to another country. This opportunity alternately bonded, then tested, their friendship. "My bestest bud at the time and I spent three weeks together at the United Nation's Youth World Conference on Women in China. We spent half the time having a blast and enjoying being in a foreign country, and half the time hating each other. We and our mothers shared hotel rooms for three weeks straight and spent all day every day together; we really got to see each other's bad sides. But I think the experience as a whole brought us together and bonded us. We have so many great memories there, like when Nina ate shrimp eyes thinking they were olives. Well, that was a good memory for *me* anyway."

When we expose our friends to a piece of our lives and our friends return the favor, we are able to grow as people. Respecting, and welcoming, each other's differences can result in a deep regard for the world around us and our small place in it.

Homogeneous

If our friends were all the same

What would we have to say to each other?

Yawn

We'd die of boredom

Growing Together

As we grow and change as people, our friendships change also. When we are children, our friendships are based on play. As we grow older, our friendships become more complex when we face new issues. Puberty strikes. Guys enter the picture. We face troubles, even tragedies. Our girlfriends are there by our side through thick and thin. We are always looking ahead. And who else do we envision walking by our side into the future? But of course, our girlfriends.

Memories

Reminiscing about our childhood friends makes us smile, laugh, and become sentimental. While friends may have come and gone, the memories remain. When we harken back to the good old days, we become nostalgic for our girlhood friends. Keeping this in mind helps remind us to cherish these days just as much, for someday they, too, will be happy memories. Ashley remembers fun times with her girlhood friend. She remembers "spinning around and around with my friend Tracy on the swing in my backyard. I was the only kid at the birthday party who didn't get dizzy." Nikole's memories of her childhood best friend include "the lemonade stands, the movies we used to go to with our lemonade money, and the dances we made up to our favorite songs." While Nikole was out selling lemonade, Elizabeth and her friend were selling jewelry. "We made beads and pendants out of clay and had her mom drive us out to a busy street corner. She stayed there the whole time with us and made sure we were OK. Looking back, the people who bought our stuff were usually just feeling sorry for us, but we had no idea at the time."

Gabriela laughs about the harmless pranks she pulled with her childhood friends. "One afternoon, after school, my friend and I filled up a water balloon to the brim, and as we walked outside we grabbed a pair of underpants and put them on the balloon. All the neighborhood kids were in the front yard, and my friend dropped the balloon and it smashed, the water spraying all over everyone, and on the ground was a pair of soggy, wet, underpants."

Jane says her best childhood friendship revolved around Barbies. "I still remember the first time I went to Olivia's house. I walked into her room and saw her Barbie collection. Barbie heaven. I immediately told her she could be my best friend forever. Hey, I was five. My standards are a little higher now."

"Don't get me started on Barbies," Piper laughs. "I remember my friend Erica and I used to pretend like we were in high school and set up lockers and stuff. I'm not friends with her anymore. She's in my English class this year, but she's so completely different, I can't even imagine that she was the one I played with."

 Nikole and Jenny's Five Ways to Relive Your Childhood with Your Friends

1. Play duck duck goose

2. Play on the bikes and scooters in the toy store

3. Have a who-can-swing-highest contest at the playground

4. Play house—and fight over who gets to be the mom

5. Make sandcastles on the beach

Some of us are still close friends with our childhood friends. These friends have seen us through the good times and the bad, and the shared history we have with these friends is irreplaceable. Tatiana remembers meeting Lindsay in kindergarten. "We tied this girl Erin's shoelaces together. They weren't on her feet at the time, but she got very upset when she tried to put them on and couldn't. She went and told our teacher on us, and we had to sit in time out. Me and Linds, we're still really tight."

There is a catch to staying friends with your childhood friends—they know some embarrassing things about you. Some of the girls responded that their childhood friends still could tease them about wetting their pants in school, throwing up in class, and the really bad clothes their mothers forced them to wear. And they remember the childhood nicknames. Grace has a rather embarrassing nickname left over from her childhood friends. "Gravy with nuts," she admits. "My friends gave me this nickname because of a dare. I will do just about any dare that is given to me. One night they dared me to eat half a cup of gravy, which I thought wouldn't be hard at all, so I took the dare. When I started to eat this gravy I found out that they had put peanuts in it. Plus, the gravy was like a month old. I was sick for the rest of the night, so everyone decided to make fun of me for the dumb dare that I had taken. I hate that name."

When our childhood friends endure through our teen years and beyond, we have to wonder how we just knew these girls should be our friends. "I have been best friends with Leah since we were six," muses Jennifer. "My sister once said we are only still friends because we are so used to each other it would be hard to change. But I don't think that's it at all. I know if I just met her for the first time now, of all the people around, we would still gravitate to each other as friends."

Early friendships form the foundation of what we know friendship to be. When we recognize the value of our friend while sharing a Barbie, we first learn the importance of trust. When our friends poke fun at us, we learn that some teasing is a form of affection. And when our friends travel with us from childhood to adolescence, we can look forward to the rest of the trip together.

Becoming a Woman

Our bodies are changing, our hormones are going crazy, and our social lives may be even crazier. Puberty can be a major challenge to get through. Nikole expresses the importance of having friends around when you are going through all these changes. "Letting me know that they are going through the exact same thing is something that helps more than a parent or adult can. It is easier to relate to a friend who is going through the same thing you are. You don't feel as out of place when your friends are going through the same thing."

"My friends had to teach me how to use tampons and shave my legs LOL!" Maria tells us. "My mother has never used tampons and, oddly enough, she doesn't have any leg hair, so I had to have my friends teach me. That's when you know you have good friends, when they teach you how to use tampons!"

When our friends get their period before us, we anxiously await the appearance of our own monthly visitor. And when it arrives, our friends are there to divulge the ins and outs of remedies and what has worked well for them. When we get our period before our friends, we might feel alone and scared but, rest assured, soon our friends will have it too, and we can all commiserate together. "I got my period first before my friend," Aneri recalls, "and it scared the hell out of me. My BFF got it about five months after I did, and she's three months older. I have killer cramps, though, and she doesn't. I am so jealous of that." Jamie was the last in her group of friends. "I would always talk about wanting to get it over with, even though all my buds insisted it was a pain. I didn't really care. But then one day I came home and went to the bathroom, and I wasn't sure if it was my period. So I called my friend Sara and told her I thought I'd gotten my period. I thought it should have been red or pink instead of the brown it was, so I told her it was bright pink. She said, 'Oh, that's odd. You might have a problem.' I felt like an idiot."

Katelyn's friend helped her overcome her fears about having her period. "When I first got my period, nobody else that I knew had gotten theirs yet. I didn't want to have to change my pad or tampon in school because I was worried someone would walk into the rest room and know. But then my best friend came into the picture. Somehow the subject came up, and I told her that I had started my period. I told her how scared I was to have it and to have to change my pad or tampon in the bathroom at school. She talked me through it and made me realize that every girl goes through it at one point in time in their life and I should be proud that it happened to me now. She made me realize that there was nothing wrong about having my period and that I should not be worried about it at all. Since then I have changed schools, but I still have no problems with changing my pad or tampon in the bathroom. And hey, now I even give a friend a pad or tampon when she forgets one at home. And the best part about it was that I learned that I could trust my friend, and then I got to help her through it when she started hers."

Some of us go through more public rituals when we reach adolescence. Char's friends helped her celebrate her Bat Mitzvah, a Jewish coming of age ceremony. "My friends were a *huge* support when I was preparing for my

Bat Mitzvah. They let me practice in front of them and made me feel like I could do anything. My friends came with me from when I was getting my Bat Mitzvah pictures developed for the Jewish newspaper to when I was going to my final lessons, till when I was getting my hair done before the big day. It made the day easier and special knowing my friends were there."

 Lindsay's Five Ways to Celebrate Womanhood with our Girlfriends

1. Partner with a friend to do a project on a female who is brave, fearless, and strong, such as Joan of Arc or Madame Curie

2. Have a video fest with only movies about girl power

3. Don't sit around comparing yourself to models in mags because you're already beautiful on the outside; work on your inside

4. Convince your friends to sign up with you for a sports team that's usually considered "boys' territory"

5. Learn together how to do something empowering, like a self-defense class or an auto mechanics class

Stephanie was privileged to attend a rite of passage ceremony for her friend Gabriela. "Karen, Gabriela's mom, did something wonderful for Gabriela's thirteenth birthday. She had a Rites of Passage ceremony, which is a way to appreciate, support, and welcome her to womanhood.

It was a women's circle, which means only females attended. Karen and Gabriela's closest relatives and friends, including my mom and I, were invited. Karen had placed pillows in a circle on the floor. In an artistic arrangement, there were pictures of Gabriela, flowers, candles, beautiful cloths in white to symbolize maidenhood, and red expressing passion for life as a woman. There were things to represent her, such as her first teddy bear and an undershirt and baby shoes.

"Everyone was asked to bring something that represented her relationship with Gabriela. Her mother led the circle and in beautiful words described how she feels about her daughter. The women shared their experiences on how they felt when they came of age and what support they wished they had had. Then we passed a candle around the circle and everyone took a turn saying something they loved about Gabriela." Gabriela chimes in, "A few of my girlfriends, like Stephanie, said such nice things about me and gave me wonderful handmade gifts and cards. It made me feel very loved. Each person told me a secret about becoming a woman. Then I read a poem and said what it means to me to be this age. This was all very special to me. It was the most spiritual time in my life."

Stephanie continues, "It was such a meaningful experience. The women and the girls felt closer to each other after this Rites of Passage celebration. I will always remember and cherish the time of that ceremony. I hope one day to have a women's circle for myself."

Our friends help us alleviate our fears and laugh at our growing pains. They help us cut through life's confusion without embarrassment and grow to appreciate the path we take to becoming a woman. Those of us honored to have friends like Gabriela's, who go even further and celebrate our entry into womanhood, honor the sacredness of our bodies and empower us.

Family Ties

Our family members are bound to us forever; these are the people who have known us since we were born. Some of us are close to our families; others fight like enemy soldiers. Those of us who consider our family members to be friends are very fortunate indeed.

Franni considers her mother one of her very best friends. "My mom always understands what I am trying to say. I tell her everything about me, even stuff she might not really want to know. She also laughs at my stupid jokes, even if they're not really funny. We have the closeness best friends share."

"I definitely consider my mom one of my best friends," agrees Jessica R. "I fight with her more than I do with anyone else, but I think that's because we're alike in a lot of ways. She's always there for me when I just need to talk and let out anger and sadness when my friends aren't around. When I was younger, I never told her anything. I was very private. I'm not sure when I finally started opening up, but I'm really glad I did. She just listens to all my problems and gives me her wonderful advice because, of course, she has been through it all. She's like my own personal therapist. Sometimes I worry that she thinks I just use her when I have a problem and need to talk. I don't want her to think that I only love her because she's a good listener. I love her because she devotes so much of her precious time to me and sacrifices a lot for me, and I try to tell her every day how much I appreciate her."

Cecily appreciates the lessons she learns from her mother. "One quality my mother has brought out in me is to help me overcome my vanity. When I was tying my hair back for karate class, I was wondering if this cute boy would notice that my hairpins didn't match. When I asked my mother, she said, 'If anyone does notice, that will not change your wonderful personality. You are outgoing, caring, and have a wonderful sense of humor. Anyone who puts mismatching hairpins over that isn't worth being friends with.' I have never forgotten this advice."

Stephanie shares a very close relationship with her mother. "Whenever I need something, my mom is always there for me. Some of my favorite times with her are when we are alone. We talk and laugh together, and she makes me feel loved. I really enjoy her company. Whether I'm sad and need cheering up or just want someone to talk to, she gives me her full attention. I enjoy talking to her so much because she listens and doesn't judge. We have our disagreements and occasional fights, but for the most part we get along and are very close. I'm sure homeschooling has something to do with how close we are because we spend a lot of time together. When we have a conversation she really respects my opinions. Some people I know treat me like I'm a child. I don't like to be talked to in a babyish way; it makes me feel overpowered and like that person has no respect for me. My mom treats me like an equal; I really appreciate being treated like I'm a human being. It makes me feel confident and good about myself. If I have a question she always tries to answer me honestly, and when she has a question for me I try to do the same.

"My mother takes us ice skating and skiing. We visit nature preserves, art, science, and living history museums, factories, and organic farms. We enjoy blueberry and raspberry picking, reading to each other, preparing food, and bird watching. On top of that she is also our teacher. Even though I enjoy spending time with my friends alone, I also love to come home and spend time with my mom.

"I really appreciate that when she's having trouble with something she's working on, she asks my opinion. Whatever my answer may be, she respects it, whether she agrees or not. If she happens to like my answer, she always gives me credit for it. I'm always touched when she likes my opinion. It makes me feel very helpful. In a way my mom is my best friend, yet I love and cherish her more than a friend because she's my mother, so I get two for the price of one."

Mothers aren't our only family members we count among our friends. Many of us consider sisters to be girl-friends. Sisterhood can be a strange relationship. We love her at times, but sometimes we just want to wring her neck and draw a chalk line down the middle of our shared bedroom to keep her away. Sisterly friendship is truly something precious; as family, she will always be there. As a friend, she understands exactly where we are coming from when we have a problem. And even though we have our moments, we will always, always love each other.

Angel considers her older sister a friend. "I can totally trust her to keep things quiet when it comes to Mom. Plus being friends with your siblings can always come in handy! She is so much fun to hang around with. Even though sometimes you have to remind her that you aren't so little anymore."

"My sister, Erin, and I have been best friends our entire lives," says Rosemary. "She's twelve and I'm almost sixteen. She is the sweetest girl I know. Because we grew up in the same setting, she and I are very similar. We are extremely close and share a relationship envied by many of the sisters I know. I love Erin very much, and I would do anything to protect her. I am so proud of her. Erin really looks up to me, and I know she's proud of me too. Our admiration for each other is just one of the things that makes our relationship so good. More so than many of my friends, Erin is a great confidante. We can tell each other anything not only because we trust each other but also because we are friends at home, not friends at school or anywhere else, and we'll never know all the people that our sister is talking about.

"Because we're around each other all the time, Erin and I know each other better than we do just about anyone else. We have about a thousand inside jokes. We love to play and pretend together. When I'm with her, I feel my youth really bubbling to the surface. She makes me laugh more than anyone else ever could. Erin and I are always smiling when we're together. Erin supports me in everything I do, and I do the same for her. She is the world to me. When I kiss her goodnight every night, I just know how precious she is and I remember how much I love my best friend for life."

Kristin and her sister Alisa are extremely close, and both had the opportunity to be interviewed for this book so neither "would miss out on the fun." They stay close despite their age differences. One way they learn about each other is by passing a notebook back and forth to each other. "We keep a notebook and write letters back and forth. I know that I can rely on her to keep a secret or not tell or show anything I don't want her to. Some of the things that are in our notebook are what we did that day, our feelings about things, what we learned at school, and who we made friends with. But Alisa mostly talks about her boyfriend."

 ## Five Relatives That Can Make the Girlfriends List

1. Moms and stepmoms
2. Sisters
3. Grandmothers
4. Aunts
5. Cousins

Sydney didn't always consider her sister a friend. "When we were younger, Jessica and I never got along. She would beat me up and do horrible things to me, and I would cry, tattle, and pull her hair. But as we grew older we realized that it's better to be friends with each other than to hate each other. So now we're pretty close. She's my friend because she's pretty much gone through almost everything that I have and can give me advice on boys, friends, parents, and such. She's going away to college, and I'm really gonna miss her."

Other female relatives outside of our immediate family can validate us. "My Aunt Patti and I are very close. I can tell her anything, and I know she won't judge me. She takes everything I say seriously, and she never belittles my feelings. We hang out and talk, and it is great to have an adult to be able to turn to," Alisa says.

Christine considers her grandmother one of her friends because "I tell her everything that is going on in my life, and she is always there for me whenever I need her to be. She never looks at me any different, and she doesn't treat me like a little kid like the rest of my family does." "My grandmother is a good sounding board for my problems," says Jenny. "She told me this story about how her boyfriend was talking with his ex-girlfriend and she got jealous. In art class, she went over to the girl and dumped her container of paint on the girl's head. She got suspended for doing that, but she said what was worse than even that was that she was ashamed for being so petty. I keep that advice in mind."

"Besides being my best friend, Marina is also my cousin," Marianna says. "In fact, she's more like a sister to me than a cousin. We grew up together, and we've been through so much over the years. No one else can understand me better than Marina. We are extremely alike, even though we may not look like it. I am as white as snow and have dirty blond hair, as opposed to Marina, who has a dark complexion and brown hair. We look completely different, yet our personalities are totally the same. We listen to the same music, hang out with the same friends, go to the same places, like the same clothes, and the same type of guys. I love Marina very much and will do anything for her. We are always there for each other, through the bad times and the good times, because that's what being best friends is all about. We've both been through so much together, surviving puberty, bad breakups, and family troubles. She's the only one from my relatives I feel I can confide in, because she'll keep my secrets. Marina and I share a bond that I would never want to give up. We'll always stay cousins, but friends, I hope, we'll stay forever."

While we can't choose our family, we can choose to have our family become friends. We share a bond deeper than any other: blood. Friendships wax and wane, but family is a constant in our lives. Being friends with our family is a gift that will give and give throughout our entire lives.

Boy Talk

It's the guy thing. The number one topic girls say they talk about with their friends is guys. The teen years are the years when our focus often turns to the opposite sex. Whether friends or boyfriends, figuring out how to have relationships with them can take up much of our thoughts. And who do we turn to for advice? Of course, our girlfriends.

Ami had a crush on a guy and was stumped as to what to do until Liz stepped in. "When I was in eighth grade I had a crush on a guy. Liz, a very cool, pretty girl in the popular crowd, taught me to flirt and instructed me about what to wear. But she'd warned me in advance that I'd hate this guy. And when I got to know him, I agreed; he really was a jerk. He asked me out and I said no." It might not have worked out with the guy, but Ami gained a new friend from the experience.

 Advice Your Friends Gave You about Guys. . .
That You Have Since Reevaluated

1. Stay away from boys; they're all disgusting.

2. Boys have cooties.

3. Boys don't like smart girls.

Of course, not all of our crushes will be reciprocated. But they still can be fun. "My friend Megan and I have a crush on Justin Timberlake. She and I will go to the store and buy the same poster or magazine because he is in it. I think having a crush on the same celebrity with your best friend is fun because you can tell each other all the gossip you've heard about him and get excited when he's on TV."

Marianna realized that she was becoming romantically interested in her guy friend and turned to her friend for advice. "I was in a dilemma. This guy was nice, charming, and a really caring friend. I appreciated everything he had done for me. He stood by my side through hard times and always made me feel better. I liked that he was so sweet and caring. But I didn't know whether I should tell him about my feelings for him. I was scared it might jeopardize our friendship, and I just couldn't take that risk. When I told my best friend, Anna, what I was going through, she told me straight up that I should tell him how I felt. She said she was pretty sure he felt the same way about me and that he wouldn't turn me down. She said he was the sweetest guy in the world and I would be lucky to date him. Anna reminded me of all of the things he had done for me and made me realize that he did like me. She said if I didn't do something soon, I just might lose him to another girl. If I handled it right, we could always stay friends. I was still pretty shaky about the whole idea, but thanks to Anna, I became more confident. That did it. I didn't want some other girl to snatch him away, so I took her advice. I told him the truth. Then he told me he liked me too, and now we are seeing each other. I am so lucky to have a friend like Anna because she helped me build my strength and confidence."

Friends often see when things are going wrong in our lives and try to help us get back on track by giving advice.

Kristin's friend helped her to slowly see the light about a guy who wasn't good for her. "I was in a relationship for a year, and he wasn't what you would call a 'winner.' We would break up because he would lie to me and then get back together over and over again. My best friend would give me advice when I asked for it and would be there for me no matter what. She did not like him at all, but was willing to put up with him until I realized what a loser he was. She knew that I was going to have to learn for myself. But her advice sunk in finally, eventually."

Our friends know us so well they can often see what is good for us more clearly than we can. When we listen, we can learn. We can give thanks for friends who care enough about us to give us the advice we need to hear.

Helping Us Survive the Breakups

These years are a time for testing new relationships with guys to see what works and what doesn't. When it doesn't work out, we seek refuge with our friends. When we suffer guy agony, the very best girlfriends jump into action. Melissa shares how her friend Susan was there for her. "When my first boyfriend broke up with me, Susan went over to his house and talked to him for me. She held my hand through it all; she never left my side; she dried my tears and made me smile."

Nikole's Five Ideas for a Valentineless Valentine's Day (with your best friend, of course!)

1. Act out your favorite girly movie—not a love story—complete with cheesy props.

2. Make valentines for your friends. Make! Not buy!

3. Bake cookies—put in some red food coloring for pink ones!

4. Prank call your crushes, or just call and wish them a Happy Valentine's Day.

5. Plan for your future with Mr. Right and how you won't settle for less.

Allison shares a story of how her friend Kate unselfishly understood the pain of a first breakup. "My friends are the absolute best for helping me with guy problems, and I have so many guy problems. The first major breakup that I ever had was the weekend of my best friend Kate's birthday party. I was *such* a party pooper because I was heartbroken, but they all came to my side and spent a lot of the slumber party trying to make me feel better. Kate dropped her place in the spotlight immediately, and they all came to my side as soon as they realized how distressed I was about it. And Kate never even cared. She was so willing to help me with my problem that I think she almost forgot it was her birthday! I felt awful, like I'd ruined her party, but she didn't even give it a second thought."

Our friends can help put our guy problems into perspective. Nikole's friend Brittany helped her regain her self-respect after a breakup threatened her self-esteem. "Brittany is my guy advice friend. She gives straight answers and opinions. My first boyfriend broke up with me. I had a lot of trouble with that. I thought less of myself than before. She cheered me up and made me believe in myself again. I wanted to get him back and be able to say no, but she convinced me he wasn't worth any more of my time." Brittany helped her realize an important lesson, that our self-worth is not wrapped up in what a guy thinks of us. And, as Pixye's friend tells her, "Men are like buses; there's always another one coming."

Sydney's friends helped her through a major breakup. "When I was depressed because my boyfriend and I had broken up, they were there for me the entire three months that I cried myself to sleep and during the day. I thought that I might drive them all off with my nasty attitude and depressing comments, but that only made them stronger friends. The fact that they never would give up on me just made me realize how wonderful they are and that I will never forget them. I was planning on spending the summer all by myself because I was really sad. I just wanted to crawl up and sleep until school started. But they forced me out and about and made me have fun, and I am really glad that they did because not only did I have the best summer of my life, but we cemented our friendship and that means so much to me now. I wouldn't trade it for anything! 'Always together, never apart, maybe in distance, never in heart,' that's what I always think of when I see them."

Marianna tells how she and her friend helped each other through breakups at the same time. "Erika and I were experiencing bad breakups from long-term relationships. We were both very depressed, but Erika was even more depressed than me. Her boyfriend had meant a lot to her, and she felt that her world had collapsed. I also had been in love with my boyfriend, but I have been down that road before and did my best not to become too depressed. I started to move on with my life. Erika, on the other hand, fell into a deep depression and couldn't get out of it. I knew I had to do something to help her. I decided we could deal with this together, and we started our journey to recovery. Every weekend we would get together and discuss our feelings freely. Since we had both been through this common experience, we could understand what each other was going through. The best medicine was to deal with it together. As months passed, we both helped each other to stop feeling lonely and sorry for ourselves. When she did feel sad, she knew she could always come to me and we would deal with it together."

When we suffer heartbreak, our friends give us their shoulder to cry on. But, most importantly, they don't let us wallow in our misery. They remind us of what is good and strong about ourselves and help us move onward — and upward.

Guy, Interrupted

Ideally, when our friend becomes happily involved with a guy, our friendship would only get better. After all, true friends want to see each other happy. But in the real world, one of the most common strains on a friendship is the introduction of a new guy. We have a best friend — and then a guy comes along and suddenly becomes her world. She spends all of her time with him. If she is not with him, she is thinking about him. When she is with us, she is talking about him. Suddenly, we feel like a second-class citizen.

Alisa's friend Stella has been there, done that. "Stella blows everybody off for her boyfriend. If she thinks that she has a chance to see him and she already made plans with you, she'll ditch you in a second. We have all come to accept this about her because he is her whole world. There was this one time when Stella kept insisting that she wasn't going to call him because she had to prove that she was stronger than that. That was when she hung out with me for the whole weekend. But it didn't last long." Sarah also has a friend who blew her off for a guy. "It was sad because my other friend and I helped her ask the guy out and be with him in the first place. Then she left us to be with him. But, not even two weeks later, she was dumped and came crawling back to us."

Laura tells us how being blown off has damaged a long-term friendship. "It really hurt me at the time that she would forget about our three-year friendship for a new boy she had just found. Every time I would want to do something with her or need to talk to her about a very important issue that was bothering me, she would always be with her boyfriend. It was like I was second now and she would only have time for me when she and her boyfriend couldn't be together. When my boyfriend and I broke up, I really needed my best friend to be there for me, but she wasn't. Now she is trying to come back, admitting that she did something wrong and saying she's sorry for not being as good a friend to me as I was to her. Things still aren't completely the same between us. My advice is don't ditch the people you care about the most in your life for someone who might not always be around. Your friends are gonna be the ones who are there for you when that boy dumps you. So it wouldn't be a good idea to leave them — cuz if you do, who are you gonna run to when your boyfriend is gone and you have no friends?"

We usually love it when we share the same taste in things as our friends. However, when we share the same taste in guys, the situation can become a problem. Angel describes how she and her friend's interest in the same guy has damaged their friendship. "I spent the night at my friend's house. We were talking about who we liked at school, and I said I would write a note to the guy she liked and help him to ask her to homecoming. Well since I started talking to him, even though it was about her, he ended up liking me. He asked me to homecoming instead. Worse, I had developed a crush on him as well. Let's just say the friendship hasn't been the same between us, really. The guy moved and, well, boys just aren't worth the loss of a friendship."

Jessica's friend went beyond the call of friendship duty in this story. "I am fortunate to have a friend like Liz who was mature and strong enough to give up this guy she liked so I could go out with him. For a few months, she had a crush on one of her guy friends but knew he didn't like her back as anything more than a friend. This depressed her, but she tried not to think about him. Then Liz had a big dance party, and I met her crush, Evan, there. I guess he took an interest in me at the party because a few days later he called me. We talked for a while, and he said he wanted to see me again. I told Liz this, and she sounded really happy for me and encouraged me.

"But then things started getting more serious between Evan and me. We went out a few times, and Liz could tell that this was going somewhere. I told her that I really liked Evan, and I wanted to continue to see him, but only if it was 100 percent OK with her. I told her our friendship was not worth putting on the line because of a guy. She said she was somewhat jealous, but she had pretty much gotten over him. She said her jealousy about the situation was taken over by her happiness for us both, and she said I should continue to pursue him. He and I are now a couple, and that is thanks to Liz. She could've been immature and selfish about the whole thing and just gotten depressed and angry because he didn't like her back, which would have prevented us from having a relationship. But she didn't. She was mature and sensible, and she realized that she and Evan weren't meant to be anything more than friends. Her selflessness made two other people very, very happy, and I'm very, very grateful to her."

LaKeisha emphasizes that she won't let a guy come between her and her friend again. "I liked a guy, and my best friend knew it. But we found out he liked her instead. I got really mad at her. I told her she probably flirted with him or something, which wasn't true. I was just jealous. She told me that if I wanted to break up our friendship over something she didn't even do then that was my problem. She was right; I was being dumb being mad at her when she didn't do anything wrong, and over a guy who didn't even like me in the first place. Never again."

Susan confessed that she can be the cause of friction in her friendship over her feelings for a guy. "This is a bit embarrassing, but it's me who causes the 'guy rift.' My friend Amy and I both have a crush on the same guy. We have gotten into fights about him sometimes because she thinks I put him above her, for example, and she thinks I would rather sit with him rather than her, etc. Sometimes, I do wish I could hang with him—only him. But Amy has made me practice what everyone knows when you're a teen, 'Friends are more important than guys.' She continually reminds me that guys come and go, but friends are there to stay!"

 Char's Top Five Songs to Put on a CD Mix for Your Friend When She Is Dumped

1. "He Wasn't Man Enough for Me" — Toni Braxton (this would help her realize she deserves more)

2. "Ex-girlfriend" — No Doubt (this would help her see how her ex hurts many girls)

3. "So Good" — Destiny's Child (this would help her see that she can move on, do well with her life, and her ex will see how much he missed out on)

4. "Heartbreaker" — Mariah Carey, featuring Jay-Z (this would help her realize he is just a player)

5. "Free" — Mya (this would remind her to be happy that she is single; she can find a great new guy who is much better or just have fun)

Lean on Me

When the going gets tough, we rely on our friends. Our girlfriends are the ones who stand by us when a crisis strikes. Having a friend's support can make the difference between a sense of hopelessness and the courage to hang on. Jamie's friend Liz helped her through a terrible time in her life when her parents were having problems. "When I was twelve, my parents divorced because of my father's two-year affair with his coworker at the school I was attending. Because they both worked there, many of the students knew, although I was in the dark. None of the students mentioned it to me. But when I found out from my mother, all the friends I'd made that year were wonderful. My friend Liz especially supported me. She invited me over whenever my parents were arguing, and we'd pass every weekend with a movie, bowling, or dinner at a restaurant to take my mind off things."

Franni's classmate lost her mother to cancer. "The day she came back to school, we had a second memorial service for her mother. I went in not thinking I was going to cry, but not knowing what the teachers had in store for us. I sat next to Mallory. The teachers told us we could go light a candle as a memorial. Pretty soon, the tears were running down my face. Mallory and I squeezed each others' hands and just cried together. I will never forget that moment."

Sydney feels grateful that she could help her friend when her friend's father died. "In my junior year of high school, my friend's father died. She was just fourteen. She had also lost her mother when she was only about a year old. She is the sweetest person, and I just felt awful for her. I went to the visitation with her, and I got out of school to go to the funeral because she said all she wanted was her friends. It was really sad because she had to make all the plans and call everyone since all her other relatives were busy. I know that she's still sad about it, but she always talks to me when she needs to. She told me that I helped a lot because I didn't just say 'It'll be better soon.' I told her that I *knew* it was going to hurt and she would want to die and she would hate God for a while but He took her daddy away because he wanted to share him with everyone in heaven. And someday she would see him and her mom soon, happier than ever because they would all be together again. I think I helped a lot, and I sure hope so. I hope that she knows she can always count on me."

Kate suddenly came down with a serious illness, and she found out who her true friends were. "The old cliché is true: Nothing shows you who your true friends are like hard times. My real friends are the ones who stuck with me when I got really sick, when nobody knew what was wrong or when I'd get better. They were the ones who wrote to me when I was too sick to even see them or get out of bed. I looked forward to those letters. I looked forward to the blue stationery and scrawling handwriting of Jamie, who always told me the details from what Mr. Arnold said in fourth period biology to what she ate for breakfast. I looked forward to the jokes and the pictures. And I cherished the cards and letters from Suzanne, who knew me best and whose notes always went deeper than the breezy epistles of my other friends. I still have every one of those letters, and I still have every one of those friends."

"One of my good friends got ovarian cancer during our freshman year," Moon tells us. "There were times when I'd be visiting her in the hospital, and she was happy despite the fact that her chance of dying was better than her chance of living. I felt embarrassed for feeling depressed about things that were nothing compared to what she was going through. I wrote her poems of happy dreams, candy canes and lollipops, and swimming all day without ever getting purple lips. But I wish I could have done more."

When Trinity felt she couldn't handle life anymore, her friend Kat helped her regroup and remember her worth. "Kat stood by me when I was in a psychiatric hospital and rehab. She wrote me almost daily and even though I was an hour away, she made me feel I was still part of her life. When no one else cared, Kat did. Kat saw me and my best and my worst. In the end, everything worked out, and Kat was part of the solution." Trinity is working on her emotional strength and credits her friends for helping her get better. "Kat and Lindsay both encourage me. They both know that one day I will be OK, and they make me feel that way too. The love is all there. They keep me going. They make the world seem less mean. Kat will drive to my house with paint, and we'll draw and paint for a while. Then she drags me out to shop or scout boys, and it makes the heavy part of life seem less important. Lindsay can't do things with me because she's in Jersey and I'm in Pennsylvania, but we talk online and on the phone. She lets me cry when I need to. With the two of them, I have both parts: the doing and the talking."

At our lowest moments, our girlfriend appears. Like a guardian angel, she comes when we most need her. Like a guardian angel, she hovers over us, offering encouragement and support to guide us through the pain.

Not My Fault

She sat there and we cried together
and I knew it was all my fault.
The way they split,
the way he left.

He got weekends and a few weeks every summer
and I knew it was my fault.
She told me "No it's not, they tried,
and they couldn't keep it together."

They screamed about me,

and my grades,

and my friends,

because it was my fault.

But Ivy said, "No! No!

They yelled about bills,

they yelled about life,

but it was NOT your fault!"

As the tears streamed down my face,

and my pillow was soaked,

she held my hand and nodded,

"My dearest friend, it's not your fault."

And I knew that when the whole world could be against me,

Ivy would always be there.

She could get through to me,

It was Not My Fault

—Nikole

When Death Parts Us

The death of a friend is one of the greatest tragedies of life. We grieve the loss of someone so young, and we also grieve the friendship that will remain only in the past. The times we could have shared in the future are no more. Our feelings swing from shock, to guilt, to anger, to grief. The stories that follow are a tribute to these beloved friends.

One of Allison's best friends died when she was only sixteen. "When I was a sophomore, one of my friends, Josephine, died. She was such a wonderful person. I don't think that I remember ever seeing her angry at anyone. She was nice to the entire school, and when I look back, I don't think there was anyone at school who didn't know her. She was so outgoing and friendly. When I was in marching band my freshman year, she and I would get up, along with several other band members, and dance during football games, even though it got us in trouble. She was just so much fun and so full of life. At the very beginning of my sophomore year, she was with a couple other of our friends, and a drunk driver ran into the surrey that they were riding in. She was killed. It was such a waste. The world is worse without her."

"When my best friend died," Laura reminisced, "I didn't know what I was going to do. I didn't want to believe it.

It was just too weird to think of life without her. She was the only person who brought me up when I was down. I always considered myself an ugly girl, but she would always tell me that I was beautiful and that I shouldn't put myself down like that. She would tell me about how when I ended high school, all the guys would be going after me and that I would have a date to every dance. She wasn't just an ordinary friend, one you would pass in the hallways at school or one who would tell you gossip about how Sally likes Bobby or Tommy is asking Chris to the dance, but she was a one-of-a-kind best friend."

Joy and her friends supported each other when one of their friends died. "I had a friend named Duncan who killed himself. He was this amazing kid who was just the most phenomenal jazz musician, but he was really depressed. None of us really saw it, but when do you see it? We went to his funeral, about ten of us. We all sat together in one row. In the middle of the services, my friend Risa leaned over to me and said, 'Remember on Duncan's birthday, when he was walking down the stairs to hang up balloons, and he fell and was just like, I'm oooookaaaaaaaaaay!' and we started cracking up. Then our friend Alex was like, 'Why are you laughing in the middle of the funeral!' and we told her. Then she started laughing. And within a few minutes our whole row was laughing about funny things Duncan had done. We didn't really feel bad because we were remembering him in a good way."

Tasha keeps the memory of her friend Brianna alive. "The day I found out about my friend's death, I had been out most of the day. There were three messages on our answering machine. All of them were from my friends — which wasn't too surprising. Two out of the three I just shrugged at and figured it was too late to call, except when my friend Jay left a message. I knew at that moment something was seriously wrong, considering he hadn't called me much before and the sound of his voice was a bit frightening. I called the number he left, and my friend that left the first message, Sara, answered the phone. I remember saying, 'Sara, what's going on?' She asked if Shannon, the one who left the second message, had told me what happened, and I said, 'No.' Shannon was then put on the phone and told me that my friend Brianna had died the day before, before the prom had started. I was incredibly stunned. I kept asking, 'What happened?' Shannon told me it seemed that Brianna had purposely missed a turn on the road. I had lost my friend to suicide. I was devastated and crying up a storm. My mother and father tried to calm me down and say that everything was going to be OK.

"I couldn't stop crying for at least three hours, and then I fell asleep. That was a Sunday. Come Monday I didn't want to go to school and face the people that would be happy while I was so sad. I went anyway and ended up staying in the guidance office with a few other friends. We were all talking about her and how great of a person she really was. At the wake I tried my best to stay calm. I went in before Jay did and looked at Brianna lying in the casket. I could see the tons of makeup they had on her face that made her look older than she actually was. Her hair was styled differently than how she usually wore it. She looked so much like a glass doll, so fragile, so not like herself when she was alive. I had kept thinking as I looked at her that it wasn't her, it couldn't be her. I stayed with my friends for the rest of the night. A group of us got up in front of the people and sang her favorite song, 'Rose.'

"I now keep her pictures up on my wall along with the poem that Jay selected for her. I visit her at the grave every now and then; the group of friends that we all share still get together and talk. I know now that the friends I have helped get me through the past two years. I see how precious they really are and hold them even closer to my heart. I still remember the Friday before Brianna's death, sitting outside my classroom in the hallway and watching her walk by, stopping her to ask what she was doing that weekend. Finding she had plans, I said we should go do something on a weekend that she had free. I think of the brilliant smile on her face, the way she had her driver's side window open no matter the weather outside, her laughs, her generosity, how she looked so happy even though she might be having a really bad day, and how she always made you feel so much life when you might be feeling down. I remember all of that and always will. She was my friend and always will be. I will honor her memory by living my own life to its fullest and by appreciating my friends who are here with me on earth."

We will always remember our friends who have died, and they will always stay young to us. There is no way to replace a friend who has died—no one will ever fill the place they keep in our hearts. But when we feel like we can't go on without them, their spirit gives us the strength to live life to its fullest, if for no other reason than to carry on what they couldn't share with us.

Dear Friend,

Life you lived was all grand.

Smiles you smiled were bright as the sun.

No one felt down with you around.

Your laugh echoes through the breeze in the spring.

Nothing has been forgotten, nothing will ever be.

The place seems so cold now.

No laughter and no cheer.

We have been surviving your sudden end.

It's what we have to do.

But we all miss you my dear friend.

—Tasha

Dreams

Our friends help us remember the past, and they help us dream about the future. We all have hopes, plans, and goals the years to come. When we share these dreams, we expose our innermost selves. We risk being laughed at, ridiculed, or told we will never be successful. But when we have a friend who supports our dreams and cheers us on toward them, we might be inspired to go beyond what we thought was possible.

Marianna and her friend Ella have their eyes on high-profile careers and encourage each other to think big. "We like to discuss our future plans as one of the most important parts of our conversation. Ella wants to go into law, and I think she will make a hell of a good lawyer. Knowing about her intellect and her accomplishments, I think she'll end up at Harvard or Yale. I, on the other hand, want to become a journalist or writer. I dream of taking over *The New York Times* someday. Ella supports what I want to do as much as I support her."

Cecily and her friend Ann share a passion, and future plans, for the theater. "One of the careers I dream of is being on Broadway! Being in a traveling theater troupe, something like that. Ann also loves to sing and act, and we can talk about our dreams without worrying that the other person will laugh at us. We encourage each other, invite each other to come see shows that the other person is in, and yet we never get competitive. It's so nice to have a friend who does the same thing I do! I think it would be great if we got cast together in something like *Guys and Dolls*, *The King and I*, maybe *The Phantom of the Opera*, anything with two leading female roles!"

Jessica R. has a few friends with whom she shares her future plans. "Of all my friends, I've noticed that only a few are interested in talking about their futures. I think this is because some of them don't know what they want to do with their lives yet. I think they feel partially embarrassed talking to me about it because I already know what I want to do with my life. I want to be an actress and attend a performing arts college. I don't want my friends to feel like they can't talk to me about their future just because they don't have any strong interests yet. I want to help them find themselves and be there when they decide what they want to do.

"Recently, my friend Stephanie and I have begun talking about our futures. She and I are both in the ninth grade and are planning on homeschooling through high school. We've been talking about the process homeschoolers have to go through to get into college and how we've already begun preparing. Stephanie doesn't yet know what she wants to be, but she knows she wants to go to college. I'm really glad that I have her to talk to about this until our other friends start thinking about it, too."

Four Ways Ella Is Helping Marianna Fulfill Her Dreams

1. She encourages me to continue writing and trying to publish my work, so I can become a successful writer someday.

2. She helped me get set with volunteer work at a near by hospital this summer, so I can help people.

3. She is helping me to create a web site that will help a lot of teenagers who are sick with Chronic Fatigue Syndrome.

4. She encourages me to help those less fortunate than me, so I can learn to help people as much as possible forthe rest of my life.

When a friend recognizes our potential and tells us that she has faith in us, we know that she is truly a girl-friend. One of Jessica's best friends wrote this in her birthday card: "You're the maturest fourteen-year-old 'woman' I know. You're gonna get far in life like that. Just think of the day when you win your Oscar and get up on that stage . . . look for me in the audience, I'll be the one raisin' the roof! If you ever have a problem, whether it may be with a guy, a friend, whatever, I'm here for you, like you always are for me. Thank you for being such a good friend to me . . . OK, enough with the Oprah moment, let's get to the point . . . Happy Birthday! Your BFF, Lisa."

Our friends not only help us dream about our futures, they can help us work toward achieving our dreams. Like Marianna and Jessica R.'s friends, they can brainstorm with us to make plans to reach our objective. No matter how lofty our goals may seem, our girlfriends are there to say, "You can do it." And they hope to be there every step of the way.

Friends 'til the End

When a girlfriend touches our hearts in such a way that no other has, we just know that we will be friends 'til the end. We picture ourselves in one another's future. We dream and plan together. We know that nothing–neither distance nor time–will keep us from being girlfriends forever.

One of the experiences that looms in many of our minds is going to college. For those of us who plan to leave home and perhaps go far away, the prospect can seem less intimidating if we plan for it in advance with our friends. Just the thought of going to college with our friends, sometimes realistic, other times not, can help us prepare for the big event. Sydney and her friends share the goal of going to the college of their choice. "It's a big decision, where to go to college. My friends Megan and Megan and I basically want to go to the same college, but Keely wants to go somewhere as far away as possible. I feel bad because I am going to miss her, but she is really supportive of us so, of course, we are of her! She and the Megans mean a lot to me so of course I want them to do whatever makes them happy. And that is all I want in return."

Rhiannon's friends also talk about going to college together—in style. "My group of friends and I have been together since the seventh grade. We keep talking about going to San Diego State together and getting a big beach house. It's a total dream life, but hey! That's what dreams are for! We all do at least plan on going to college, and we support each other in school and in trying to keep our grades up."

We also imagine our futures beyond the college experience. Getting jobs, getting married, having children—all topics of speculation among friends. Melissa and her friend Markie imagine each other as the maids of honor in each other's weddings. "Or maybe we will even have a double wedding!" Melissa says. "We already have our wedding colors, and dresses, and everything picked out."
"My friend Hannah says we're going to make sure we get pregnant at the same time so our kids will get to grow up as friends," Jenny says. "She'll be the godmother of my kids, and I will be the godmother of hers. We'll take family vacations together to Disney. I can picture us sitting on the beach surrounded by all of our kids and still being as close as ever."

And we think onward even farther into the future. FF! Friends Forever is a major rallying cry among girlfriends. We can envision our lives as older women, holding on to our girlfriends through decades and decades. "As my friend Marina says, 'We laughed together, we cried together, and we'll die together!' That's a little too exaggerated, but I've always believed a true friendship won't die out," laughs Marianna.

Ami pictures herself in the future this way: "Aggie and I will be friends forever, despite our numerous differences. I can see us, sitting in her home in Seattle, sipping tea, ordering our kids and grandchildren around. We'll be on her massive porch, which will have lots of potted plants and a swing chair, and we'll both be wearing these old lady dresses. We'll have old photos and stuff across our laps (we both love taking goofy pictures) and of course yearbooks and stuff and old résumés, which we'd have shoved into shoe boxes over the years. It'll be raining, and our kids will be inside, worrying about us, and we'll get up and run around and dance in the rain, on the street, with no coats."

"Elaine and I see ourselves sitting on a couch in some little apartment in New York City, watching TV and talking about how 'those darned punk kid actors can't act' and 'they've lost all respect for the arts entirely,'" laughs Joy. "I've written a few poems about it, and Elaine and I talk about it sometimes. We think we'd be really funny if we were old together. We want to be rockin' grannies that do cool stuff and are just as boisterous in their old age as they were as kids."

Trinity has a vision of her forever friend. "Lori and I will be sitting in rocking chairs, with our grandkids biting at our ankles, asking us stories about what it was like growing up in the 1900s, saying that they cannot believe we were able to survive with the technology of the early 2000s. We'll both have walkers, that are never used, sitting next to us, and we'll be talking about my latest fling. Our grandkids will watch us use language in utter disbelief because by then there will be no face-to-face talking; talking will all be done by little computers and such. Lori and I will make jokes, and I will continue being totally random. In the morning I'll fly over to her house (by then no one will walk, might as well join the trend), and we'll share tea, with crackers and cookies on the side. Then the day one of us dies, the other will die too. And we'll be buried next to each other."

Forever Friends

it's that long and winding

road

that always leads

to your door where i know

I'm always welcomed in.

it's that future we have planned together

it's that question you always ask me:

"what will we be like

when we're older?"

well,

i don't know.

but i know that

we'll still have

each other.

not a wrinkle,

not a cataract,

not a bad hip,

or a wheelchair

can take that away

from us.

because

our bodies might change,

but our friendship will stay

the same;

it's that

that keeps me going.

—Joy

Being friends forever doesn't mean never fighting, arguing, or losing touch for a couple weeks—-or even years. We will all face the challenges of a relationship in each friendship we foster. The friendships that last forever outlast temporary troubles. We see past the problems and recognize that under it all, our friend is still there, supportive and loving as always. And the phrase "Friends Forever" really will come true.

What Is a Girlfriend?

friend *n.* 1. attached to another by affection or esteem; 2. a favored companion. *Synonym:* pal, buddy, companion, acquaintance, amigo, confidant, familiar, intimate, mate, associate

While teens have many definitions of what a friend is, the qualities of a true friend—a girlfriend—have common themes.

A girlfriend is trustworthy. "A friend is someone who you can trust, and she can trust you, too" says Ami. "A friend is someone that you can tell your deepest, darkest secret to and know that no one will ever find out about it because you would trust them with your life," Christine describes. "A true friend will tell you things no one else would, things that aren't sugarcoated for you, but will tell you even if it may hurt your feelings. She is someone who can tell you if you look fat in those jeans, but doesn't really care if you do," Angel adds.

A girlfriend is there when you need her. "A true friend is there for you when things are going great as well as when things are not," says Faith. "If something horrible were to happen to you, she would be there in a second to comfort you, to hold you, and to help you heal. A true friend doesn't let you down. She is someone you can count on." Allison says, "A friend can even be the girl that you talked to once because she saw you crying and asked you what was wrong. Maybe you never saw her again, or never talked to her, but she was there for you, so for a minute, she was a friend. A friend is someone that, when you break down in tears, she's there for you. A friend does not think less of you for crying, no matter what. A friend will be there for you through rain or shine, thunder or wind, and would do just about anything for you, so that you could be happy."

A girlfriend is loyal. "A true friend is someone who sticks with you through thick or thin," says Jazzi. "She stays with you when everyone turns on you. She sees you through bad times as well as the good."

A girlfriend respects you. According to Cecily, "A friend is someone who does not invalidate your opinions, no matter how much she disagrees. A girlfriend supports you, even if she does not agree with your course of action or thought, unless it is truly wrong. She needs to share your views on many things, but disagree on a few. When that happens, and if a debate starts, she should do it thoughtfully, and with respect for your opinion."

A girlfriend encourages you to higher limits. "A friend always encourages you to do your best and helps you to never give up. A friend is someone you can share your dreams with," says Alisa. "A true friend is genuinely happy for you when it goes your way. She cheers us on when we win the game, helps us make it through the speech without throwing up," responds Jennifer. "A friend always pushes you to go far and be all you can be. She helps you think on the bright side. A friend will do everything in her power to help you succeed."

A girlfriend likes you for who you really are. "A friend is someone who you can feel comfortable acting stupid around," says Devon. "Someone who can tell you the truth without hurting your feelings. Someone who you aren't afraid to show your true self to, and you can kick back and relax with." Jamie describes it this way: "A true friend is someone who likes you for the person you are. She doesn't judge your past, and she isn't critical of your personality. She doesn't betray you or purposely hurt you in any way. She doesn't try to always be better than you or more popular than you. A fake friend is someone who just uses you to get ahead. She's someone who doesn't really like you, and she wouldn't mind hurting you if it helped her."

A girlfriend listens. Cassie puts it this way: "A girlfriend is a person who listens when you really need to talk. She doesn't just use you when it is convenient. She wants to hear what is really going on with you and how you really feel. You can confide in her and know your secrets are safe. A friend is someone you could call at any time like at one o'clock in the morning, and she'll understand how you feel if you just got dumped by your boyfriend." Rebecca says, "You cry to her and she'll stay on the phone listening to you, trying to give you advice and talking to you to make you feel better. And then she'd expect you to do the exact same thing when something horrible happens to her." "If you don't have friends to talk to about problems, they are just going to build up inside you and eventually they are going to explode," notes Patricia.

A girlfriend gives as much as she takes. "With a girlfriend, there is a back and forth friendship going on, it's not just a one-way street. Good friends give you their shoulder to cry on, but then you give them yours back," says Aneri. "When you do things with a true friend," explains Melissa, "you take turns. We pick things we know the other would like to do too, so she won't be bored out of her mind. After all, a friendship is a little give and a little take."

A girlfriend is laughter. "A friend is someone who you can act completely goofy with and can count on to go along with weird Lucy-and Ethel-type schemes with you," says Katie Lou. "A true friend is someone who gets the joke," says Jessica. "Who you can laugh with until your cheeks hurt, your throat is raw, and you don't even remember why you are laughing anymore."

A girlfriend is safe. "Friends give us a sense of belonging," says Melissa. " We all have that moment where we walk into a party and feel like we don't know anyone. Or we walk into the cafeteria on the first day of school and wonder where to sit. Then we see a friend, and a rush of relief washes over us. We know where to go."

❇   ❇   ❇

Endnotes

1 Sara Shandler, *Ophelia Speaks: Adolescent Girls Write about Their Search for Self* (HarperCollins, 1999).
2 Susan Wilson, *Sports Her Way: Motivating Girls to Start and Stay with Sports* (Fireside, 2000).
3 Dr. Carol J. Eagle and Carol Colman, *All That She Can Be* (Simon and Schuster, 1993).

About the Author

Julia DeVillers is a freelance writer and the coauthor of several books. She is the former editorial director of a health education publishing company, where she developed books and multimedia for teens. She has a master's degree in journalism from The Ohio State University and a bachelor's degree in communications from SUNY Oswego. She currently lives in Columbus, Ohio. She stays home with her two young children and writes books at night. Writing *Teen girlfriends* inspired her to track down several of her long-lost friends from her teen years in Albany, New York. She has had reunions with them in several states and online.

About the Press

Wildcat Canyon Press publishes books that embrace such subjects as friendship, spirituality, women's issues, and home and family, all with a focus on self-help and personal growth. Great care is taken to create books that inspire reflection and improve the quality of our lives. Our books invite sharing and are frequently given as gifts.

For a catalog of our publications, please write:

Wildcat Canyon Press
2716 Ninth Street
Berkeley, California 94710
Phone: (510) 848-3600
Fax: (510) 848-1326
Visit our website at www.wildcatcanyon.com